HUMANISM AS THE NEXT STEP

HUMANISM
AS THE NEXT STEP

by

Lloyd & Mary Morain

HUMANIST PRESS

WASHINGTON, D.C.

First edition © 1954 by Beacon Press.

Printed and bound in the United States of America.

Library of Congress Catalog Card Number: 2008920462

ISBN 978-0-931779-16-9 (paperback)

Contents

INTRODUCTION

Humanism, a Joyous View

Could you be a humanist without realizing it? Perhaps you have been looking for a meaningful philosophy of life that is in harmony with mature intelligence. Humanism is an alternative to traditional religious faith and is in tune with the growing knowledge of our physical and mental worlds. And now, when many long-held ideas no longer seem relevant, it provides a new source of joy, strength, kindliness, and morality. Rational thinking and its handmaiden science can free one from guilt brought about from giving lip service to ideas that are not really believed. And it can end the feeling that life is just a waiting room at the entrance to heaven or hell.

Humanists understand that there is no supreme power with a human face that controls us. They know how problems can best be solved by perceptive, rational thinking. They have found that, with a better grasp of the processes of the world, personal lives become energized and more meaningful. Humanists share in the discovery that the meaning of life is that which they give to it. They gain access to a more full-bodied excitement as they feel closer to nature and become a part of all that lives. Vision is wedded to knowledge, and a sense of freedom lets each day become more exhilarating, more of an adventure.

This is the philosophy of evolutionary biologist Richard Dawkins, philosopher Daniel Dennett, social critic Barbara Ehrenreich, journalist Michelle Goldberg, novelist Joyce Carol Oates, evolutionary psychologist Steven Pinker, novelist Salman Rushdie, politician Pete Stark, magician James Randi, comedian Julia Sweeney, business leader Ted Turner, writer Gore Vidal, and biologist Edward O. Wilson. This was also the philosophy of the late entertainer Steve Allen, science fiction author Isaac Asimov, sexologist Mary Calderone, psychologist Albert Ellis, inventor R. Buckminster Fuller, paleontologist Stephen Jay Gould, actress Katharine Hepburn, biologist Julian Huxley, elder citizens' advocate Maggie Kuhn, anthropologist Ashley Montagu, civil rights leader A. Philip Randolph, philosopher Bertrand Russell, astronomer Carl Sagan, birth control pioneer Margaret Sanger, novelist Kurt Vonnegut, and other thoughtful, constructive people of the twentieth century. Becoming free from outworn dogmas has opened many to greater understanding, new insights, and a more rewarding life.

Today, in an increasing number of nations, an increased and more humanistic sense of inclusiveness has supplanted the notion that relationships between genders, classes, and ethnic and national groups are eternally fixed. The domination of women by men has been recognized as rooted in ancient religions. Millions of people have come to realize that most of the turmoil in the world has been fostered by those holding onto and fighting for outmoded dogmas. Consider the situation in much of the Middle East, where people are divided into rival Muslim sects, following their banners as they destroy their neighbors. If most everyone in what is now the Islamic world were an agnostic or an atheist, would there be such strife?

Moral inconsistencies and social agonies throughout the world can usually account for the widespread retreat to religious fundamentalism at one extreme and the narcotic escapism of some New Age structures at another. Meanwhile, traditional mainstream religions still cannot fully accommodate current knowledge and belief or meet emotional needs.

So humanism is a true alternative. But not everyone who has acquired a humanist outlook has automatically felt drawn to use the humanist label. Nor have all sought to become part of a humanist organization. But those who have made this choice find value in having a clear identity and in being part of a community of the like minded. It can be enjoyable and often useful to join at least occasionally with others who understand and feel much the same way. Moreover, individuals of all social and cultural proclivities can feel they are not alone in their humanist point of view.

As a life philosophy, humanism brings together the subjective and the objective. It furthers moral values and prepares a person to accept change. And asserting the value of the human adventure, it provides purpose and meaning to life and energizes the motivation to carry on.

Acknowledgements

Many thoughtful individuals have made helpful suggestions that aided in the completion of this book. Without the inspiration of Alfred Smith and the conscientious attention of Fred Edwords and Karen Hart, this book would have remained unfinished.

Many other people have, in one way or another, stimulated the thinking of the authors. Ideas which blossomed in the works of Oliver Reiser, Edward Ericson, Brock Chisholm, Porter Sargent, Warren Allen Smith, Abraham Maslow, Alfred Korzybski, Bertrand Russell, and Cora L. Williams were often in our minds.

Of course, there were innovators who developed slants and programs that influenced our attitudes at significant times. Among these were Roy Fairfield, Garrett Hardin, Fran Hosken, Arthur Jackson, Edna Ruth Johnson, John Kessler, Beth Lamont, Gerald A. Larue, David Loye, Pat Maginnis, Stephen Mumford, Lyle L. Simpson, and Rabbi Sherwin T. Wine.

There were and are the adventuresome innovators with unique and often glorious humanistic ideas, some of which are yet to come into their own. Here we were indebted to Joseph Ben-David, Norman Fleischman, LeRue Grimm, Mel Lipman, Michael McOmber, Francis Mortyn, James W. Prescott, Pearl Ross, and Roger Williams.

We were also fortunate over the years in being able to share our outlooks with friends. More than that, we were often able to bask in the aura of their warm common sense. Early on there were Frances R. Dewing and Cyrus Eaton, and later James F. Hornback, Lester R. Mondale, Ernest Morgan, Ward and Barbara Tabler, and Herbert Tonne.

Friends, thinkers, glorious innovators, and creative, insightful movers have all played some role in this endeavor to give an overview of the humanist terrain.

CHAPTER ONE

The Alternative to Faith

A Growing Movement

Every year more men and women of all backgrounds are calling themselves humanists. For them much in the old orthodoxies has lost significance. They are finding satisfaction in the positive, constructive point of view of humanism. It shares much with the philosophies and religions of the East as well as of the West. In Europe, Asia, and the Americas it is coming to be known as the alternative to traditional faith.

Throughout the ages religions of many kinds have contained a common spirit. We can see this in parts of their scriptures.

In Hinduism we find: "This is the sum of duty: Do naught unto others which would cause you pain if done to you" (*Mahabharata*, 5, 1517).

In Buddhism: "Hurt not others in ways that you yourself would find hurtful" (*Udana-Varga* 5, 18).

In Christianity: "All things whatsoever ye would that man should do to you, do ye even so to them: for this is the Law and the Prophets" (*Matthew* 7, 12).

In Confucianism: "Is there one maxim which ought to be acted upon throughout oneís whole life? Surely it is the maxim of loving-kindness: Do not unto others what you would not have them do unto you" (*Analects* 15, 23).

In Islam: "No one of you is a believer until he desires for his brother that which he desires for himself" (*Sunnah*).

In Judaism: "What is hateful to you, do not to your fellowman. That is the entire Law; all the rest is commentary" (*Talmud, Shabbat* 31d).

In Taoism: "Regard your neighbor's gain as your own gain, and your neighbor's loss as your own loss" (*Tiai Shang Kan Ying Piien*).

In Jain scriptures: "The essence of right conduct is not to injure anyone."

But varying religious practices and diverse theological beliefs have been built upon and allied to this common ethical principle.

Down through history humans have adopted creeds that provide special privileges and practices that separate them from other groups. Throughout the world, wide cultural variations continue. Ways of worship, hierarchies of leadership, rituals, symbols, and sacraments are different. Humanism goes in a different direction and concentrates on what we all have in common. It has become a dynamic alternative to the traditional faiths.

Among the reasons for the growth of traditional religions was the need for explanations of natural occurrences, day and night, summer and winter, life and death. Scientifically minded individuals in recent centuries have figured out the huge distances beyond our planet and have likewise revealed the amazing world of the submicroscopic. Humanists realize we now have answers to many of the questions which once were explained in ways that now seem fanciful and unnecessary.

Humanists know there are evolving and fascinating explanations to answer the questions asked through the ages; they do not need to turn to the supernatural. They feel at home in the natural world and do not need gods or a god, a heaven, or scriptures. Moreover, they feel that humans do not need the promise of a heaven after death to be just and kind to others, to feel loyalty to the whole of humanity and the environment. They respect scientific methods and the knowledge coming from their use. They want to apply this knowledge toward the care of this marvelous planet.

Humanists are content with fixing their attention on this life. Theirs is a point of view, philosophy, or religion without a god, a heaven, divine revelation, sacred scriptures, or authoritarian spiritual leaders. Yet theirs is an overarching view rich in feeling and understanding, which is sensitive to the sorrows and joys, tragedies and triumphs, touching every fiber of human life. They experience wholesome humility as they venture forward with fellow humans into the as-yet-unknown.

This rapidly growing philosophy and religious alternative:

(1) has developed in response to the spiritual needs and aspirations of people in different parts of the world;

(2) contains an ethical core similar to that of many traditional religions and philosophies;

(3) is free from divisive doctrines about the unknown, deity, revelation, sacred scriptures, rituals, sacraments, formal theology, big inequalities in social roles between the sexes, and such befuddling ideas as the radical separation of either the world or the individual into matter and spirit; and

(4) is a philosophy of human relations to one another and to nature, rather than of relations to deity.

Built on this fresh and vital basis, it is little wonder that humanism has called forth accelerated worldwide interest. In 1952, for the first time, representatives from humanist groups in many countries met in the Netherlands and formed the International Humanist and Ethical Union. Julian Huxley, a leading scientist and the first director-general of UNESCO, served as chair. He was among those who believed that the world was ready for humanism.

Here in the United States, the number of humanist

and humanistically focused organizations is growing. Some of these groups, in particular many of the Unitarian Universalist fellowships and Ethical Culture societies, are functioning under the auspices of a liberal religious denomination. Each year more and more Catholics, Protestants, Mormons, Muslims, Sikhs, Baha'is, Hindus, Buddhists, and Jews, as well as many without any religious or philosophical affiliation or desire to have one, are coming to accept this as their own way of life.

This alternative to faith is held by a large number of individuals who have made or are making solid contributions to human welfare and understanding. We can note Carl Sagan, Ashley Montagu, Riane Eisler, Steve Allen, Betty Friedan, Buckminster Fuller, Linus Pauling, Erich Fromm, Isaac Asimov, Bertrand and Dora Russell, Kurt Vonnegut, Abraham Maslow, Benjamin Spock, Alice Walker, Richard Lamm, Margaret Atwood, and Albert Ellis. In many respects humanism's strength is found in the high proportion of eminent leaders and thinkers who today hold this alternative to faith. Yet, to an increasing degree, most who follow this way of life are individuals of average accomplishments who represent a cross section of the world's population.

Mentioning some of the people who have expressed ideas consistent with this rich and varied view may help in the understanding of humanism.

Those who have contributed to the advancement of human welfare and understanding on the international scene include Brock Chisholm, Julian Huxley, John Boyd-Orr, Gerald Wendt, Margaret Sanger, and Ted Turner.

There are, of course, varied emphases in humanism, and the particular quality of an individual's views will be conditioned, within the very wide limits of this philosophy, by background, whatever it may be—science, philosophy, business, social work, the arts, liberal religion, freethought, or just by limited economic and educational condition. Some individuals do not apply the humanist label to themselves, that is, have not yet come out of the figurative closet. In some cases they may even point to a particular humanist and say, "I am not that kind of humanist." But would not that also be true of any other philosophy? A few people have labelphobia. Our list is, however, a reasonable cross section, and most of the Americans mentioned have been members of the American Humanist Association. The few who have not can be identified by their own writing and declarations as pursuing this way of life or have expressed in their published views many humanist principles.

This alternative to faith is beginning to make an impact on human affairs. Its effect is appropriate in our age in which humans are coming to realize their own strength and worth.

Ours is a time of vigorous protest, of a desire for reassurance. We see in many regions agonized efforts of peoples to rule themselves, to be free from dictators, to democratize their governments. Just as most political concepts of divine right and clerical control have been disregarded, so many of the traditional religious and philosophical ideas are being challenged. In many instances people have simply turned away from religious activity. They are doing this even in those countries where to do so can politically bring social disapproval, even ostracism. For them no institution or group of people has a corner on wisdom or on high ethical principles. It is becoming more and more evident that religion is often chiefly a political factor. At the same time more and more thoughtful people are likely to recognize the whole human family as a great interdependent brotherhood.

People everywhere are coming to realize that science makes orderly knowledge possible, as it is not limited to just local belief. They know that biologists, whether in Bolivia, Botswana, Japan, Nigeria, or Sweden, have a basis of common principles and share the fruits of their knowledge. There is no special kind of Bolivian or Botswanian biology which is radically different from Swedish biology. Political leaders in a few nations have tried to shape scientific studies to nationalistic ends but they sooner or later failed in this. People are also coming to understand that ethical principles and basic standards of moral conduct have common roots and universal application. It is only natural that those groups that limit or tie these standards to religious observances and theologies are probably fighting a defensive, losing battle. The human spirit is too needy and too vigorous to be kept in shackles.

We have seen the formation of humanist groups in nations as different as India, Norway, and Argentina. Organizations in several countries have been started by individuals who had no inkling that, at the same time, people in other countries were engaged in similar activities. Men and women in different nations arrived at the same conclusions and proceeded to form groups.

Both in the United States and in other parts of the world, humanism is thought of as an alternative force. That is, it is considered a different type of belief and action in contrast to the authoritarian political systems on the one hand and to the traditional religions on the other. Little wonder there are entrenched interests that consider it threatening or dangerous.

Whether or not there will be humanist halls in every city of our land and tens of millions of members remains to be seen. It is not essential to belong to an organized group to be a humanist. In its present stage of growth, humanism is having a liberalizing influence on many of the traditional religions and philosophies. Within the Unitarian Universalist and Ethical Culture organizations whole congregations are becoming openly humanist. The mounting concern of Buddhists and the Protestant, Catholic, and Jewish clergies over the effect of humanism on some of their members testifies to the appeal and strength of this liberating alternative to supernatural faith.

Humanist organizations are not entirely focused on

bringing people into their organizations. Many in liberal churches enjoy membership in both a church and the humanist organization. Such humanists take part in the educational and social programs which are cooperating rather than competing membership organizations. The Habitat for Humanity is one example. Human fulfillment is the goal; institutions may or may not be instruments of fulfillment.

Religion and the Religious Attitude

Attempts to ridicule religion or to dismiss it as unimportant rarely meet with any lasting success, for religion is a vital part of the lives of many, and it gives every indication of continuing to be so.

Religion has been defined in nearly as many ways as there have been definers. It is often spoken of as "a system of faith or worship," or as "an awareness or conviction of the existence of a supreme being arousing reverence, love, gratitude, and the will to obey."

Other thoughtful individuals have given very different definitions. Thomas Paine merely said: "The world is my country, to do good my religion."

A. Eustace Haydon, when professor of comparative religion at the University of Chicago, offered as his definition: "The shared quest of the good life."

Alfred North Whitehead described it simply as "what the individual does with his solitariness."

To us religion is the creation and pursuit of ideals and the relationship people feel with one another and with the universe. For us religion and theology are not equivalent words but rather theology is only type of religious expression.

Humanists are divided in the belief that individuals can have a religious experience that does not include any supernatural element. Some note that religious feelings and attitudes have been mistakenly limited to that which is becoming less and less real and meaningful to us—the old theologies and rituals.

John Dewey described religious attitudes as basically a thoroughgoing and deep-seated harmonizing of the self with the universe. And he further defined religious experience as that which has the power to bring about a deeper and more enduring adjustment to life. Can we not agree with Dewey that everyday life will have more meaning once we realize that so-called religious experiences can be a part of its fabric?

Julian Huxley regarded the basis of religion as "the consciousness of sanctity in existence, in common things, in events of human life."

From time immemorial humans have related their lives with the larger life of nature. They wished to feel that their code of social behavior had something of the sacred in it. These attitudes have been organized together in the idea of "God." Yet we can receive these same satisfactions from a philosophy that is not built on the idea of deity. We can learn that ideals are in reality useful goals growing out of human experience and not set apart from creative life. We can learn that our lives are more closely woven into the whole universe than we had even suspected in the old days. Religion without a supernatural element can become meaningful and personal. Partially because of the conflict of sects, some of us do not regard humanism as a religion but as an alternative.

The endless struggle between science and religion can die down. The spiritual aspects of life are no longer inconsistent and at odds with those things that we can experience and test. No longer need there be that type of spiritual realm that does violence to our intelligence and to our knowledge of the processes of the world. Humanists recognize that we all live in a unified world, the world of nature.

Humanism as a Philosophy and Religion

Humanism, like religion, has been defined in innumerable ways. Many a humanist has made his or her own definition. This is a healthful condition, for truths are not contained within the words of definitions. The value of definitions is in calling attention to relationships or in making appropriate descriptions. The broad general humanist viewpoint, enriched as it is by the insights of people of varying temperaments, cannot even be sketched within a few sentences or paragraphs. As it is a general point of view it is only natural that different people should find different aspects of it particularly significant to them.

Those individuals of more philosophical bent will look to it as a living philosophy. If they are technically trained they may study humanist ethics and stress the values of good morality. Some whose primary interest is found in current world problems, in revising laws and customs toward building a better, happier human community, naturally think of humanism as a point of view that could bring all the people of the world together. For them it is a challenging call to make full use of all that is in us to build cooperatively a richer human life. The interest of yet others is in the role of humanism as a champion of the rational approach over the traditional theological one, of democracy over authoritarianism, of common sense over superstition. A fourth focus hails it as a means for achieving personal integration, maturity, and freedom. Once these personal values are won, concern in and action for the larger social good follows naturally for all of these groups.

Whether or not one looks to humanism as a religion, as a philosophy, as a lifestance, or as a way of life is, we believe, largely a matter of personal temperament and preference. Those caught up by its religious aspects know that it provides a vibrant, satisfying moral orientation. Those who think of it as a philosophy find it both reasonable and adequate. Those who recognize it as an alternative to religion may or may not feel personal value in belonging to an organization.

One of the great religious humanist pioneers, John

H. Dietrich, pointed out:

> For centuries the idea of God has been the very heart of religion; it has been said "no God, no religion." But humanism thinks of religion as something very different and far deeper than any belief in God. To it, religion is not the attempt to establish right relations with a supernatural being, but rather the upreaching and aspiring impulse in a human life. It is life striving for its completest fulfillment, and anything which contributes to this fulfillment is religious, whether it be associated with the idea of God or not.

Humanism gives to many people the satisfactions which have come to them in the past either from other religions or from other philosophies. In doing this it serves some as a religion, others as a philosophy. Insofar as it serves as both a philosophy and a religion, there is no need to deny that it has both functions. Inasmuch as faith in a theology is not involved, it can be recognized appropriately as an alternative to faith.

It developed as the rational scientific viewpoint was grafted upon a philosophy of good will and concern for humans and nature. It is neither vague nor colorless but positive and dynamic, whether thought of as a non-sectarian religion, a philosophy, a lifestance, a way of life, or an alternative to faith.

CHAPTER TWO

Forerunners of Humanism

Seven Contributing Ideas

The ideas that make up modern humanism have developed slowly throughout history and will not fade into oblivion just because people may some day cease to use the term "humanist." Although there were individual humanists throughout the world in each of the past fifty or more centuries, it has been only in recent ones that these ideas have been recognized as forming a point of view, an approach to life.

There are, however, certain specific ideas which have gone into the making of modern humanism. Seven of these, although at some points shading into one another, seem to us to stand out.

As a starting point let us take the idea that this life should be experienced deeply, lived fully, with environmentally sensitive awareness and appreciation of that which is around us. Those of artistic or venturesome inclination, in particular, have had this keen awareness. This earthy state of mind has existed throughout the ages, particularly in many tribal societies.

Another idea is that nature is thoroughly worthy of attention and study. Early philosopher-scientists, among them Aristotle, shaped this notion.

Still another idea is that of confidence in humankind. For expression of this we are indebted in large measure to the to the eighteenth century democrats who had faith that humans can control their own destinies.

A fourth idea is that of the equality of rights among humans. This is part of the democratic ideal and for it we are again particularly under obligation to the eighteenth century democrats. More recently anti-slavery and women's movements have come to the surface.

Cooperation and mutual aid can be thought of as a fifth central idea. This important theme lies deep in most religions. Early humanists were exhilarated to see it given a new justification through the work of sociologists and biologists.

A further idea is that of evolution as worked out by nineteenth century scientists. Early humanists were quick to realize the implications of development through gradual change.

For a seventh and last idea we have chosen scientific thinking, the need to demonstrate a theory by testing and experience. From this has been built the whole modern rational scientific method of verification by experiment. Perhaps no other idea has been of more practical importance to the humanist movement than this one.

Enthusiasm for Life

Back through the centuries whenever people have enjoyed the sights and sounds and other sensations of the world, and enjoyed these for what they were—not because they stood for something else—they were experiencing life humanistically. Whenever they felt keen interest in the drama of human life about them and ardently desired to take part in it, they felt as humanists.

The Greek and Roman philosophers Epicurus and Lucretius urged their followers to find happiness in the present world, in nature, and in the affection of friends. During the Renaissance there was a general rebirth of interest in the present, of zest for living.

In each age the work of some writers and artists has revealed the beauty and harmony of the world as it is, beauty that might otherwise go unnoticed. Such work has given new insights into the grandeur and meaning of human life as we experience it. Beethoven's fifth and ninth symphonies, Rembrandt's portraits, Shakespeare's plays, and Lou Harrison's multicultural compositions do this for us.

Nature Matters

Throughout history many have used their intelligence and energies to force nature to give up its secrets. They have done this in order to make life more livable, or because of an inspired, disciplined curiosity. Indians in North and South America and many Asian and African societies focused on understanding and interacting with the soil, sky, and whatever grows and lives.

In the humanist tradition are Copernicus, Galileo, and other investigators who, in the face of indifference or hostility, courageously observed, experimented, recorded, and formulated. Scientifically focused, they took the whole universe as their domain, daring to explore the heavens, the earth, and even humankind.

Protagoras, speaking in Greece in the fifth century Before the Common Era, encouraged people to turn their minds to the investigation of what lay about them. "As to the gods," he said, "I have no means of knowing either that they exist or do not exist. For many are the obstacles that impede knowledge, both the obscurity of the questions and the shortness of human life."

Many centuries later Francis Bacon, leading the revolt against medieval scholasticism, urged people to be rational, to look at the world more scientifically.

In philosophy, the materialist and naturalist tradition had sturdy roots in ancient Greece. Early philosophers based their systems entirely on the natural world in founding schools of thought. The naturalists emphasized the sufficiency of nature as a framework for thinking. The materialists developed theories of matter that, in general outline, are little different from those held in modern times. Today these have been developed and blended together. But they barely survived the rise of the Church and the advent of the Dark Ages. In the Western world the modern tradition can be traced through Francis Bacon, Baruch Spinoza, and Charles Sanders Peirce to George H. Mead, John Dewey, Arthur Bentley, and Julian Huxley. Modern refinements have been important but, for this school of thought, nature as the sum total of physical realities still remains the framework.

Late in the nineteenth century Robert Green Ingersoll told thousands of Chautauqua attendees what few had been taught to believe:

When I became convinced that the Universe is natural—that all the ghosts and gods are myths, there entered into my brain, into my soul, into every drop of my blood the sense, the feeling, the joy of freedom. . . . For the first time I was free. I stood erect and fearlessly, joyously, faced all worlds. And then my heart was filled with gratitude, with thankfulness—and went out in love to all the heroes, the thinkers who gave their lives for the liberty of hand and brain. And then I vowed to grasp the torch that they had held and hold it high that light might conquer darkness still.

Confidence in Humankind

In the Western world during the Renaissance there was manifested a new confidence in human powers, but the social implications of this new awareness were first fully faced in the eighteenth century by those who fought for human rights. These leaders felt confidence in what all people could do if given freedom. They had a profound belief in reason, a deep distrust of all tyrannies which control our minds.

These individuals lived in a world where political, economic, and religious power was in the hands of a few. They lived in a time when the dead hand of tradition was strong and that tradition backed by deeply entrenched interests. Classical scholars and priesthoods encouraged respect for divine revelation and discouraged self-reliance. People were told to accept rather than to investigate and to question.

Through the centuries religious leaders had taught that there were laws beyond the reach of reason and that one should follow obediently those who knew and interpreted such laws. They taught that we should concentrate on reaching the next world rather than center thoughts and actions on this one.

We see here two opposing moods: the one for self-determination; the other against it. As John Herman Randall, Jr., has said, history is an alternation of two moods . . . there is the mood of supernaturalism . . . a mood of dependence and self-abnegation, a bitter realization of frustration and failure, in which man's confidence oozes to nothingness and he feels himself the plaything of forces which he cannot pretend to comprehend.

And there is the humanistic hope "involving the triumphant apotheosis of man, the creator and builder."

The eighteenth century democrats Jean-Jacques Rousseau and Voltaire believed in liberty. They felt that only where people are free are they able to become all they might be. Thomas Paine and Thomas Jefferson were opposed to all governments, institutions, laws, and customs which restrained the free use of our minds, which imposed arbitrary, unnecessary authority on how we shall think and act.

Thomas Jefferson wrote:

> I am not an advocate for frequent changes in laws and constitutions. But laws and institutions must go hand and hand with the progress of the human mind. As that becomes more developed, more enlightened, as new discoveries are made, new truths discovered and manners and opinions change . . . institutions must advance also to keep pace with the times. We might as well require a man to wear still the coat which fitted him when a boy as civilized society to remain ever under the regimen of their barbarous ancestors.

Equality

We are indebted in large measure to the eighteenth century democrats not only for their concept of political freedom but for the idea of political equality. Not only is there intrinsic value in each of us, but there is a basic human equality among us.

Political and religious leaders traditionally supported the theory of divine right and the notion that some groups were inherently superior to others. Some people with an independent turn of mind—nonconformists who were perpetually getting into trouble—looked at all the kings, dukes, bishops, and priests and whispered the simple questions: What, if anything, makes them superior? What indispensable purpose do they serve?

Mutual Aid

For centuries many religions have advanced the idea that all men are brothers and therefore should help one another. This notion, however, has fared but poorly and still is bravely struggling for survival in a largely callous world. The difficulty lies, perhaps, in that humans have been told merely that it is a duty to feel as brothers and sisters. We have been given no satisfactory reasons.

There are, however, many reasons why the modern humanist is convinced of the value of cooperation. In the first place, concentration of interest in the present, in this life on earth, acts as a dynamo generating the idea that existence should be tolerable for everyone. If this is the only life we can be sure of, let us make it a worthy one, both for ourselves and others.

During the last hundred years, furthermore, the humanist knows that scientists have made clear how cooperation is, in a very real sense, important to survival on many levels of life. Pyotr A. Kropotkin pointed out how crucial to human and animal survival is the exercise of mutual aid. At least one paleontologist found in cooperation the grand strategy of evolution. According to H.M. Bernard's zoological researches, the development of higher forms of life was made possible by the progressive cooperation of cells.

Things Evolve

Many early Greeks, Asians and Africans did not believe that the world had been created as of a particular date by a deity. They felt that somehow this universe with its wealth of living things had changed or evolved from some simpler forces and material. Certain nineteenth century scientists had come to this view but not until the publication of Charles Darwin's *Origin of Species* were average men and women faced with the idea of evolution.

In early consideration of this discovery most felt that a common ancestry with animals lowered the human race to a level with them. There were others, however, who sensed that in the idea of evolution there lay cause for special encouragement. While other living things must adapt themselves to nature, must change their own forms, humans on account of their special gifts are able to adapt nature to themselves. The idea that we can consciously turn the process of evolution to our own advantage, to further our own good, to recreate the world and ourselves, is at the very center of present-day humanism.

During the nineteenth century a few thinkers suggested that moral laws have not come to us through revelation. Herbert Spencer's strong voice announced that these are the results of our experiences in living with one another and are not the precepts of any supreme being. Here we find emphasis on the evolutionary aspect of morality. This too contributes to our philosophy.

Experience Is Our Guide

Gradually we humans have learned to test the truth of our notions by experience. Within recent centuries this practical good sense has developed respect for rational thinking and the scientific method, a method which has served the interests of humanity more successfully, more humanely, and therefore in a sense more spiritually, than any other. Within the past century some of the implications of this method have become widely known and appreciated. Most citizens of the technically advanced countries have at least a vague faith in the practical results of scientific approaches. However, there have never been large numbers who perceived how much value there was in using this method in one's own daily life, or in the building of a living philosophy. Those who were able to see it as a major tool in their total adjustment to life have been, to that extent, in the humanist tradition.

And So—Humanism

By the twentieth century many individuals, impelled by their own kind of interest in the world around them, had been carrying on a quiet revolution. They had built up for us an entirely different picture of the universe—and of our place in it—from that which had been accepted in the Middle Ages.

The established religions—Christianity, Islam, Judaism, and to some extent Buddhism and Hinduism— had been built around a predominantly static picture. The new picture is so different that many have been repelled or have not been able to bring themselves to accept it. It was the impact of this new knowledge, however, which brought about the transformation of humanism into a relatively clear-cut body of ideas and into organized movements. Humanism has developed as scattered individuals and small groups realized that they had a common bond in their thorough, ungrudging rational acceptance of new knowledge and its implications.

Let us consider certain of the changes brought about in knowledge during the past few centuries.

The earth, this globe of ours, once proud center of the divine handiwork, has lost considerably in geographical importance. Even our sun, itself 109 times the diameter of the earth, is found to be but an average-sized star on the edge of a galaxy of perhaps 300 billion other stars. Beyond this there are likely more than 100 billion other galaxies!

The earth, once thought in Europe to have been created about 4000 BCE, is now known to have a far longer history. It is recognized to have formed 4.54 billion years ago and has reached its present condition through a series of changes and continues in a process of evolution.

And humans, once center, master, and darling of the universe, for whom all else was created, have had to take a more humble position. We have evolved from earlier forms of life and differ far less from our closest living relatives than had previously been supposed.

Moreover, the findings of advancing knowledge reveal that each of us is an inseparable unity of body and mind, of thought and emotion. The "soul," long believed to be a human's unique possession, has evaporated into literary metaphor.

When the impact of this new picture was first felt, the implications seemed staggering. How could people accept the new view of humans and their universe? We had lost our security, our importance, we who had been the favorite sons and daughters of the creators! We who were made for a special destiny! Some even feared that our most precious human goals, values, and ideals would lose importance in this new world.

But these implications did not stagger the humanists of a century ago. They had a solid confidence in humanity. To them humankind needed no privileged position in the scheme of things. Having a genuine respect for, and interest in, human purposes and human ideals for their own sakes, they were not upset to find that these are not linked up with any great purposes of the universe as a whole.

Far from shrinking from the implications of biology, anthropology, astronomy, psychology, paleontology, and physiology, they made them the basis of their thinking. They built up from them the philosophy and lifestance of humanism.

The sociologist Frank H. Hankins pointed to humanism as becoming a logical step in the human venture:

Sociological and historical researchers have shown that the essential core of religion is devotion to those social values which bind men together in cooperative effort for group preservation and mutual welfare; and that these values are discovered through human experiences. Among those discovered in recent times are devotion to truth as exemplified in the scientific mentality, the dignity of individual man, and the ideals of democracy. Humanism thus becomes the next logical step in religious evolution; it is the heir and creative fulfillment of the Renaissance, the Reformation, and the democratic revolutions.

CHAPTER THREE

Some Basic Beliefs

The Fundamental Premise

Basic to humanism is a particular approach to the world about us—to the physical and psychological environments. This approach or method is considered more important than any conclusions reached by using it, for knowledge is continually increasing. Conclusions about many things in the world have to change as knowledge grows. It is necessary to remain open minded, to avoid jumping to conclusions, and often to suspend judgment. When we form a conclusion it is important that we do not force it upon other people. Whereas in most religions and in some philosophies certain matters have been laid down, accepted on faith, and held to be true for all time, this is not true in humanism. We hold in high regard the scientific method—the constant search for information and the willingness to change opinions as warranted. Even when speaking of morals and ethical values, the humanist makes few assertions and likes to point out the context.

To clarify further the difference between the method of which we speak and the one used by those who base their belief on faith, pioneer American psychologist

Frances R. Dewing, in a letter she wrote to the authors, says:

> One of the essential things about scientific method is an open mind, critical only of the quality of the evidence, and a readiness to accept any conclusions. With this goes an eagerness to find the principles that can be used to give us successful dealings with our objective experiences. These principles as long as they work are what we call truth.
>
> Contrasted with this basis for truth which assumes dependence on reasoning power there is truth by authority—personal, organizational or "by the book."
>
> This cleavage of method is a more fundamental cleavage than cleavage according to items of conclusions, especially as by our method any conclusion is conceivably possible. The only negative allowable is the denial of the right of any other person to assert a statement without showing reasons—especially to assert truth for others dogmatically.

Humanists generally hold views on mind, heaven, immortality, essences, and the ideal that are hard for anti-naturalists to understand. Some of these concepts will be discussed later on, but here we wish to point out that they are not the heart of the naturalist alternative. In fact, sin, heaven, immortality, and deity are considered rather unimportant ideas.

Points of General Agreement

How we believe is more important than what we believe. Because we use the scientific method we recognize that even our most central beliefs may have to change in the light of further evidence.

It would be strange if thoughtful and independent people did not have differences of opinion concerning the most significant ideas in their common philosophy, if there were no real disagreements as to implications and emphases. The naturalist alternative, many-faceted, humane, experimental, has room within it for many varieties of opinion.

On some points, however, there is general agreement. Let us consider certain significant ones:

(1) Humans are, in every respect, a part of nature. They are a natural product of evolutionary processes.

(2) We humans, like all other living things, must rely upon ourselves, upon one another, and upon nature. There is no evidence that we receive support or guidance from any immaterial power with

whom we might imagine we commune.

(3) We are able to meet the challenges of life in constantly more satisfying ways provided we are able to make fuller use of our capacities.

(4) The meaning of life is that which we give to it. Happiness and self-fulfillment for oneself and others are richly sufficient life goals.

(5) Moral codes are made by humans. Values and ideals grow out of the experience of various cultures, societies, and individuals.

(6) The supreme value is the individual human being. Each person, of whatever race or condition, merits equal concern and opportunity. Laws, governments, and other institutions exist for the service of men and women, and are justifiable only as they contribute to human well-being.

Believing in the capabilities of humans to solve their problems, having confidence in the scientific method, in experience, in knowledge, and in the natural creative processes of the universe, the humanist feels that humankind can successfully make better todays and build toward a better tomorrow.

Humanists in Action

Bette Chambers, one-time editor of *Free Mind*, the membership publication of the American Humanist Association, often summarizes phases of humanist endeavor. In 1996 she reminded her readers of significant social-action successes:

> In the last half of this century, we've seen abortion rights established by law. Many states have recognized—or are in the process of recognizing—individuals' rights to choose the manner and time of their demise. There has been increased sensitivity to women's roles in the home and the workplace and decreased tolerance for sexual harassment. We've witnessed the legal establishment of civil rights for persons of color and opportunities broadened for all minorities.
>
> These humanistic changes did not come about in a vacuum. Humanists and humanistically inspired individuals, as well as socially conscious organizations like the American Humanist Association, have fought long and hard to achieve them. Our 1957 Humanist of the Year, Margaret Sanger, went to jail to champion

birth control. Patricia Maginnis, our 1978 Humanist Pioneer, was also incarcerated for fighting for abortion rights. Dr. Henry Morgentaler, our 1975 Humanist of the Year, pioneered abortion rights in Canada and was arrested, jailed, and acquitted three times. Dr. Jack Kevorkian, our 1994 Humanist Hero, has endured and been vindicated in four trials in the pursuit of ending the suffering of individuals through physician-assisted suicide.

Find an important victory in the humanization of our society in the twentieth century, and you'll find Humanists—often AHA members—leading the charge. In time, fair-minded people of traditional faiths joined in these causes, but it was Humanists who first laid their lives and fortunes on the line, going to jail or bearing social opprobrium until public dialogue led to these reforms.

CHAPTER FOUR

Answers to Some Common Questions

Are Humanists Agnostics?

Some humanists would call themselves agnostics whereas others prefer the term atheist. But not all such nontheistic individuals qualify as humanists.

Humanists do not have what James H. Leuba called "a God to whom one may pray in the expectation of receiving an answer." Professor Leuba added, "By ëans\werí I mean more than the subjective, psychological effect of prayer." They find no evidence in the universe of any non-human personality which is concerned for the welfare of the human race.

However, they recognize that God is thought of in a wide variety of ways. The term God is applied by some people to nature, by others to love, by others to goodness in humans, and by still others to the grand design—the way things work in the universe. A humanist does not necessarily reject a very impersonal idea of God, but feels that there are more fitting ways of expressing these aspects of nature.

Although humanists have a nontheistic point of view,

it does not follow that all atheists and agnostics could be described as humanists. Agnosticism or atheism is a relatively unimportant part of humanist philosophy. One can be an agnostic or atheist and hold to good ethical values, but atheists and agnostics can also show cruelty in life, or indifference toward other humans. Many humanists dislike the labels of atheism and agnosticism because they know that humanism involves much more. What they do not believe counts relatively little; what they do believe and how they act on their beliefs make them humanists.

But humanists don't replace worship of a god with worship of humanity, because humanists do not worship in the traditional sense. To be sure, the fulfillment of human life is their highest value and their goal. But they realize that this fulfillment is dependent upon human inter-relationship with other varieties of living things and nature as a whole. They know that nature and its laws largely set the course and determine the goals humans must seek to be fully human. Their needs, their hopes are developed in interaction with each other and nature.

How Do Humanists Use Sacred Scriptures?

Some humanists find inspiration in the scriptures of Buddhism, Confucianism, Islam, Christianity, and other religions. These humanists are students of the Bible or other religious texts and may hold them in high regard.

For some, the story of the historical progression of the people in the Middle East from belief in tribal gods to belief in a world god can be inspirational. The Christian Bible, Quran, and other sacred texts, however, are not regarded as authorities in matters of belief and morals. But many stories attributed to the Buddha, Lao-Tzu, Mohammed, Confucius, and Jesus are humanistic in spirit and purpose. Whether or not all religious stories and myths are true does not necessarily matter so long as they serve as useful guideposts for some people.

For example, Jesus can be viewed as a great ethical leader. To the work of the previous Jewish prophets he added a special insistence on the place of love, kindness, and forgiveness in human life. Humanists do not attribute divinity to great religious leaders but often find inspiration in their lives and teachings. They believe that the ways of life they taught, or which are attributed to them, have often been obscured by creeds and rituals, and that fundamentally their teachings were concerned with human relations and with the daily practice of social virtues.

What Is the Humanist Basis for Morality?

The humanist basis for morality is found in the study of human beings. Actions are evaluated in terms of their consequences.

The humanist usually looks with favor on the ethical

codes of the traditional religions, but points out that in different cultures there are wide differences of opinion as to what is moral.

For centuries the roles of men and women in most New Guinea tribes were well defined and observed. Women planted the food crops, looked after pigs, and took care of the children. Men took care of guard duty, participated in tribal clashes and maintained the cultural practices, which called for much philosophizing.

During the Second World War, there was an influx of Australians and American military troops. Tribal warfare was pretty much ended, and the cultural "heavy thinking" which was the men's province was generally discredited. As could be predicted, philosophy lost out along with warfare. Today the women are still rearing the children and working to raise and provide food. Men seem to have less to do and in their lowered status can be observed looking for tourists or making things to sell to them. Fishing, however, is still done by both sexes.

Some traditional religions are chiefly interested in establishing right relations with God or in fulfilling mystical plans. Humanism is concerned that through intelligent cooperation we live a good humane life; that we maintain positive relations with friends and family; that we lessen poverty, war, disease, male domination, and prejudice; and that we provide opportunities for and sustain young people. The welfare of each of us is dependent, to some extent, on the welfare of all. We do not have to believe the same things but we need to recognize our common humanity and the need to keep in balance with nature's resources.

What Do Humanists Think about the Soul and Immortality?

We are constantly learning more about the interrelationships of mind and body, intellect and senses, genes and DNA, and the effect of inheritance and early living environment. We realize more fully how wonderfully sensitive and intricate is the human nervous system. No longer is it necessary to explain our best thought and feeling as the result of an inner light. There just does not seem to be any evidence of, or any need for, an immaterial soul or spirit. Some humanists do, however, use the term "soul" as a poetic metaphor. Deep and important life-giving feelings are often spoken of as spiritual.

Immortality implies the existence of a soul, a soul which can be separated from the body. We know of no humanists who believe in a dualism of soul and body.

Humanists do believe most thoroughly, however, in the kind of immortality which flows from the effects on others in the way one lives, effects which often continue long after we have perished.

In giving up the idea of life after death, we give up the all too often comforting belief that suffering and deprived fellow humans will have their miseries taken care of and made up for in another life. Humanists recognize the necessity of keeping life livable for self and others in this life.

Was Our Country Founded on the Belief in God?

No. Thomas Paine, Thomas Jefferson, George Washington, and Benjamin Franklin were all deists or freethinkers. At the time they lived, deists were considered little different from those without any belief. We do know that these founding fathers were not interested in identifying the government of the new country with a religious concept of any specific kind.

At the Constitutional Convention it was voted after some discussion that the word God would not have a place in the Constitution. Later on, John Adams, while president, signed a treaty with North African Muslims, saying in the name of the United States: "The Government of the United States is not in any sense founded on the Christian religion." Our country has become strong partly through the foresight of our founding fathers. There is no historical evidence that only a believer in a theological religion can have faith in freedom, in self-government, in democracy, or in family values. It was only in 1954 that Congress inserted the phrase "under God" in the Pledge of Allegiance.

Do Humanists Go to Church?

Some humanists go to church and some do not. In the United States, wherever there is a liberal church congregation or new thought group, they are likely to include one or more professed humanists. Among organized religious groups one is most likely to find humanists in Ethical Culture societies; in Unitarian Universalist, Congregational, and United Methodist churches; in liberal Jewish, Quaker, and Baha'i Faith congregations; and in human potential and Zen Buddhist groups. Today the members of these groups are often humanist.

Meetings of primarily humanist groups are not considered church functions. Some of these groups are, however, very little different from those within liberal religious organizations.

Families with growing children are often eager to find humanist-oriented Sunday schools which are free of dogma and help children understand ethical values, learn social responsibility, find their own answers, and make intelligent choices. Unitarian Universalist and other liberal churches as well as Ethical Culture societies offer such Sunday school and youth programs welcoming participation of humanists. The distinguished historian Priscilla Robertson gave helpful suggestions on bringing up children in a nontheistic home. More recently, Lloyd Kumley and Devin Carroll vigorously pioneered the development of nontheistic publications and activities for young people. And today the field is rapidly expanding.

Do Humanist Leaders Receive Training?

Some do. A scholarly program for training leaders for humanist groups, the Humanist Institute, has been in existence more than a quarter century. Other programs have been developed by the Center for Inquiry and the Institute for Humanist Studies. The Humanist Society offers occasional training sessions for humanist celebrants.

How Are Humanist Groups Financed?

Although in Europe some humanist organizations receive government support, in North America each group is on its own. They prosper financially through membership dues, donations, grants, earnings from investments, and the sale of products and services. Lyle Simpson, while president of the American Humanist Association in the 1980s, established the Humanist Endowment Fund to help guarantee the survival of humanism and humanist organizations into the future. It now continues as the Humanist Foundation. Meanwhile, other humanist organizations have set up their own endowments.

Do Humanists Oppose Ceremonies and Rituals?

No. Ritual and symbolism help some people to feel more deeply. For them these things make philosophy and belief more vivid and provide emotional and aesthetic satisfactions.

Humanists appreciate emotional experiences. However, they tend to shy away from rituals and symbols when they notice how often in the past these have become fixed forms, taking on more importance than the things they originally represented. They feel that symbols should not be mistaken for that which they symbolize. They are saddened to watch symbols acquire a meaning of their own and lose their significance as human expressions of work, growth, love, abundance, family, death, life, fertility, and reverence for the unity of nature. Military conflicts all too often have had close affiliation with religious symbols.

Is Humanism Less Complete than Religions?

No. Although lacking the rigid, fixed scriptures of an alleged revelation, the sources of inspiration, written or otherwise, which humanists use are very wide. Naturalism draws on all the living poetry and literature that expresses joy and hope. It cultivates the awareness of beauty, love, truth, and life. These are dynamic, ever-growing sources of feeling. Infused with these sources of inspiration, humanism offers a complete and satisfying philosophy and way of life. It not only frees one from guilt but gives comfort and provides inspiration. It helps individuals develop self-esteem, maintain personal well-being, and face the concerns and problems of daily living.

Do Humanists Claim Absolute Certainty?

No. Dogmas are avoided. As Malcolm H. Bissell, educator and a past vice-president of the American Humanist Association, said:

> For the tragedy of mankind has not been written by the searchers for the final answer, but by those who have found it. No man ever hated his brother for doubting what he himself could still question. No Columbus who *knows* what lies beyond the horizon ventures forth to find a new world. The fruitless battle of the sects has long since told its bitter and bloody tale. A thousand centuries of fears and forebodings, of priests and prayers and persecutions, have brought us only to the inscrutable stars and the silent mountains. The gods have not spoken; we ourselves must design the good society of which we dream.

Is the Humanist Way of Life a Satisfying One?

Growing numbers of people are finding it so. There is comfort in discovering oneself to be in a vital relationship with nature and with one's fellows. There is a sense of well-being which comes from cooperating with others for the common good, in recognizing universal kinship—whether or not we differ in our philosophies. This alternative to historic faith is in harmony with the growing knowledge of the universe and its inhabitants. As a dynamic, developing point of view it sustains as well as stimulates. It challenges us to free ourselves from outworn stereotypes and to live according to the highest ideals of the human race. It enables us to feel self-reliant and at home with ourselves and nature.

Has Humanism Sacrificed All Sense of Assurance?

For some people the revealed certainty and mysticism of the traditional religions has no counterpart in the humanist alternative. Others feel differently.

If humanists are without a belief in a dependable fatherly being who will protect them against nature, they realize that in another sense nature itself is dependable. As we study our environment, it becomes less frightening and more predictable. As we understand and cooperate with nature, we flourish. Ours is the assurance that no event, no experience, is necessarily beyond reason. There is a basic sort of order and explanation, if we could but find it, for whatever happens to us and around us. Investigation may well lead to discovery of activity which in turn will lead to improvement of an unwanted situation.

Humanism is built on the accumulated knowledge

of humanity so the humanist does not have to fear for a faith or be forever on the defensive against advancing truth. It gives therefore an assurance and security not available to those whose philosophy or religion is ever in retreat before the growth of knowledge. Furthermore, one is no longer burdened by trying to believe in something which one feels is not true.

Do Humanists Believe the Naturalistic Alternative Can Unite People?

Yes. The ethical codes of the great religions are very much alike, although there the similarities often end. Humanism is free from divisive doctrines about the unknown, free from rituals and ceremonies and liturgical regulations that so often separate people and set them apart from each other. There is no damnation, no purgatory, no heaven, no hell, no mystical realms or planes. But humanists can receive a deep satisfaction from being part of a total natural world. Humanism is concerned with the harmony of life on this earth we share. Historical theologies vary, as do the ways in which people aspire and worship, but the essence of these religions and philosophies—the teaching as to the way humans should behave—is often similar. In humanism this good moral life is justified in terms of our having proper relationships with nature and with each other. Humanists are united by their devotion to the scientific spirit and acceptance of differences among individuals.

Albert Einstein, in his *Living Philosophies*, published in 1933, said:

> Strange is our situation here upon earth. Each of us comes for a short visit, not knowing why, yet sometimes seeming to divine a purpose. From the standpoint of daily life, however, there is one thing we do know: that man is here for the sake of other men—above all for those upon whose smile and well-being our own happiness depends, and also for the countless unknown souls with whose fate we are connected by a bond of sympathy. Many times a day I realize how much my own outer and inner life is built upon the labors of my fellow men, both living and dead, and how earnestly I must exert myself in order to give in return as much as I have received.

Do Humanists Have God-free Ethics?

Yes. Humanists do not expect that dishonesty, bad treatment, or cruelty to others will be forgiven in a future afterlife or heavenly existence. What we do now is what matters. Concern for others becomes our salvation.

Paul Kurtz, a leading force in humanist outreach, in his book *Forbidden Fruit: the Ethics of Humanism*, notes:

> The ethical conceptions of tomorrow must

be truly planetary in perspective. We must transcend the limits of the narrow loyalties and parochial chauvinisms of the past, and recognize that basic human rights are universal in scope, for all persons are part of a community of humankind.

Caring about the welfare of others helps provide inner strength and doesn't depend upon guidance from a God. Feeling at home in the universe and the joy that comes from thinking positively does not depend upon any theistic belief.

Are There Many Nonreligious People?

Comparing figures from such resources as Adherents. com, the *Encyclopedia Britannica*, the *New York Public Library Student's Desk Reference*, and the *World Christian Encyclopedia*, one can arrive at useful estimates of the current adherents of world religions. The chart below summarizes this data with figures that add up to a world population of 6.6 billion.

Religion	Adherents	Percent
Christianity	2.1 billion	32
Islam	1.3 billion	20
Hinduism	0.9 billion	14
Buddhism	0.4 billion	6

| All others* | 0.8 billion | 12 |
| Nonreligious | 1.1 billion | 16 |

*This category includes Sikhism (23 million), Judaism (14 million), and other minority faiths as well as a wide range of folk religions.

From the above we can see that nonreligious people of various types (including agnostics, atheists, freethinkers, humanists, and secularists as well as nonreligious deists or theists) represent one out of every six of the world's people and comprise the third largest of the above groups. This reveals the global significance of non-identification with religion.

CHAPTER FIVE

How Humanism Meets the Needs of Individuals

Three Basic Needs

Philosophy and religion serve people in various ways. For some individuals these meet many of their psychological needs, for others very few. But it can be agreed that in almost all instances philosophy and religion offer at least to some extent a means of comfort, a source of ethical standards, and a wellspring of inspiration, and that by so doing they fulfill fundamental needs.

Most people would concede that the older religions offer these satisfactions. How do the ideas which are at the core of this alternative to faith give comfort, provide ethical standards, give inspiration, and provide motivation for living?

Mental and Emotional Security

Religions and philosophies have traditionally given humans a very comfortable position in the universe. We had the reassurance of knowing that we were in contact with a power beyond nature that gives the human race love and protection. Like those who sponsor an appeal for funds after any national disaster by saying, "Remember, God spared you," we knew that the Almighty had us constantly in mind.

Today we still need some kind of basic reassurance about our relationship to the world in order to know that we have a place, that we are accepted. Most of the time our friends, family, or work give us some sense of belonging. However, for many there are times when these are not enough, when we have to turn elsewhere for security. Then, perhaps feeling lonely or unwanted, many draw renewed courage and comfort from a reassuring picture of themselves in relation to God, or to a larger whole—the universe, the world, or humankind.

How can humanism give this kind of picture? How can a philosophy which questions whether there is any unique concern for the human race, either in nature or beyond it, give the equivalence of religious and philosophical reassurance?

Humanism teaches first that there is an intrinsic, inalienable value in all human beings. This is not a value that has been given us by a deity or that we hold only because we have earned it. It is our birthright. We can have a mystical and poignant depth of feeling about this, for at the very heart of our philosophy is a warmly genuine sense of the value in every human, whatever their ability, however they are circumstanced.

This can be the foundation for an invulnerable sense of self-respect. The feeling of security that comes to one who has this kind of self-respect enables one to withstand the incidence of misfortune and of disgrace. It even stands firm against those savage attacks that we sometimes level at ourselves. This kind of feeling about oneself is still appropriate even if one has become entangled in some shameful mess.

Secondly, humanism encourages us to feel that, no matter who we are, we have untapped abilities, unknown potentialities, and more strength, inventiveness, and capacity for survival and progress than we know. We are to look for strength not outside ourselves but within. Erich Fromm, in his book *Psychoanalysis and Religion*, speaks of the value of having a faith in the power within ourselves to meet life with courage. Some philosophies and religions stress how weak, how evil, and how foolish we are by nature. Although they offer a way of escaping from this lack of strength, virtue, and wisdom, they first impress on us our deficiencies. How much better it is to emphasize hope and self-confidence. How much better to know that we must and can take care of ourselves.

Thirdly, it teaches us to look for courage and for comfort to one another, to our fellow humans, of whom there are more than six billion. We all have experienced the pleasantness of a sense of closeness with a group of strangers when we suffered some minor mishap together, for instance the breakdown of a subway train between stops. Why can not this satisfying sense of solidarity be called up in all of us by the realization that humankind can expect no special dispensation from the universe? Is it not stimulating and comforting to acknowledge our dependence on one another in our unique situation within nature?

Finally, for many humanists the deepest sense of security comes from feeling themselves an integral part of nature. A. Eustace Haydon expresses this beautifully:

> The humanist has a feeling of perfect at-homeness in the universe. He is conscious of himself as an earth child. There is a mystic glow in this sense of belonging. Memories of his long ancestry still ring in muscle and nerve, in brain and germ cell. Rooted in millions of years of planetary history, he has a secure feeling of being at home, and a consciousness of pride and dignity as a bearer of the heritage of the ages and a growing creative center of cosmic life.

This sense of belonging can come to those who realize that we are in every respect a part of nature—a nature far larger, far older, than ourselves.

All through history people have been eager to have a close relationship with the nonhuman world about them. Humanism makes this relationship obvious and logical. We can feel a myriad of ties with other living creatures. We can feel an enriching expansion of sympathy and interest. Living things are fellow experiencers of life, knowing fears of rejection and injury and the satisfactions of acceptance, warm sun, food. We do not claim special privileges and are ready to face, with other living creatures, the full force of the joys and tragedies of life and death.

In years past many of nature's processes were considered entirely unpredictable and strange. The gods served as special protection against a nature often cruelly hostile. Now that we are learning through the sciences the chains of cause and effect underlying many of these events, they tend to seem less mysterious, less frightening. The idea that there is a kind of basic coherence behind occurrences gives a measure of security. The as-yet-unknown furthers new perceptions. There is a strong, deep certainty in nature's laws.

In these several ways humanism can make possible a sense of security. Certain privileges have been given up but in their place we have gained self-reliance and a closer bond with all of our fellow humans and with the universe.

Ethical Standards

A second need felt by humans is for a standard of behavior, for ethics. Behind many of the moral codes of the past has been the pressure, the force, of eternal laws, eternal rewards, and punishments. How does humanism build its ethics and standards of behavior, how does it enforce them?

Ethics in the humanist view is largely the responsibility we have for the well-being of others.

There are no inflexible rules in personal ethics, for what will be ethical in one situation will not necessarily be so in another. The question of right and wrong is a very practical one. How will behavior affect the well-being of others at a particular time and place?

Our precious social virtues cannot be pressed into the character of individuals by precepts or by authority. We should act honestly, justly, considerately because we feel that this is the natural, the necessary way to behave.

A sturdy basis for ethical behavior is self-respect. The humanist knows that if one is of value, so are others; if one has a right to happiness, self-fulfillment, so have others. And self-respect develops when an individual achieves personal maturity, when one understands strengths and limitations, and recognizes the position of men and women in the scheme of things.

Rudolf Dreikurs, a psychiatrist, expresses this thought in two of his "Ten Premises for a Humanist Philosophy of Life." He says:

> Humanity's greatest obstacle to full social participation and cooperation is an underestimation of their own strength and value. . . . The greatest evil is fear. Courage and belief in their own ability are the basis for all their virtues. Through realization of their own value they can feel belonging to others, and be interested in others.

There are ideas deep in this philosophy which encourage one to feel thus connected with, and interested in, other people.

Humanists gain a bond with others when they recognize that they must and can help one another in common problems, against common obstacles.

Humanism also provides the strongest possible motive for kindliness and consideration, for justice and honesty. If we believe there will be no second chance in a future life to make amends to family, friends, and acquaintances for the difficulties and unhappiness which we cause them, and if we believe there is no future of bliss for them but that this life we share is all they will ever know, it becomes paramount that we do what we can to make this existence a happy one.

We are not quick to condemn the simpler, more elementary enjoyments. We do not think of these as unimportant or debased. We do not suggest that the pleasures from line dancing, reading comic strips, playing video games, or even watching wrestling matches are not worth much. Happiness is a great good and we should accept it where and when it is offered to us and harms no one.

Because we do not make the distinction between an admirable soul and a less admirable body, we do not separate ourselves into two parts wherein one part of ourselves is respected while another part is scorned. We refuse to set up fierce battles between impulse and conscience and therefore there is no endless inner struggle between good and evil. The normal sex drive, for instance, is not thought of as evil in itself. Like all basic human needs it is not intrinsically wrong but can cause harm when directed in irresponsible ways.

Accounts given by anthropologists of ethics in regions as varied as Samoa, Morocco, and New England are more than merely entertaining. They show that what is considered right behavior with respect to one's neighbor or one's father-in-law is different in various parts of the world. Our standards of behavior have grown up, slowly and painfully, from the particular experiences of the group into which we happen to be born.

Aubrey Menen pointed out that early in this century any married woman in Malabar, India, who wore clothes above her waist was considered to be aiming at adultery. It was unthinkable for a cultured adult to sit eating with another, for this would require putting food into the mouth, chewing, and swallowing in public. As for sitting in one's own dirty bath water—never!

Yet societies have traditionally felt the need not only for codes of behavior but for some kind of superhuman, eternal justification for them. There has been widespread belief that what is right and what is wrong must be eternally right and wrong, and right and wrong for all. It has often been thought that unless people believe this they will think too lightly of codes and standards.

However, the realization that ethics are built up by humans for their use in relations with others is in no respect dangerous. Isn't there something appealingly practical in the notion that good behavior is that which leads to human welfare? This point of view seems the best kind of justification of and encouragement to honesty and unselfishness.

When a code of behavior is thought to be handed down from a greater power, one obeys from reverence or from fear. There is often the added incentive of punishment or reward. Humanists do not have these forms of persuasion. They like the ones they have— the expectation that people will want to follow those standards which have proved best for individual and general good, and the recognition that an individual who is mature in body, mind, heart, and spirit is eager to work for the common welfare.

And many humanists see beneath all differences in customs and codes a common denominator. They see the principle of mutual aid as a law of survival.

This, then, is part of humanist ethics.

Inspiration

We need more than ethics, more than comfort, from a philosophy or religion or alternative to faith. We need inspiration. We need to express the upreaching and inspiring impulse in human life.

Inspired by an idea or by a symphony of sensory impressions, we feel alive. Our senses dance, our spirits soar. The crusts of routine and monotony are cracked. The concerns of everyday life are seen in a new perspective, seen in terms of what is supremely worthwhile. Life takes on a new meaning. A thoroughly inspirational idea also leads to some kind of purposeful behavior. One is not only inspired but inspired to act in an unaccustomed direction or to be a different kind of person.

There is a deeply inspirational quality in humanism. Many are drawn to it because it has power to inspire them as nothing else does.

This may seem to be a paradox. How, one could ask, can a point of view inspire if it questions whether there is any absolute and preordained meaning to human existence? How can a philosophy inspire if it doubts that humans have a role to play in a moral drama transcending life and death?

Yet it is these very ideas which seem deeply, obviously inspirational to humanists.

Many years ago John Dietrich put this idea into other words for his Minneapolis Unitarian congregation:

> Although the universe cares not about our ideals and our morality, we must care for them. All the virtues and all the values, all there is of goodness and justice, kindliness and courtesy is of our own creation and we must sustain them, or otherwise they will go out of existence.

And further,

> Against the terrifying background of an uncaring universe, we may each set

a triumphant 'soul' that has faced facts without dismay, and knowing good and evil, chosen good.

Many humanists would maintain that, here, too sharp a line has been drawn between humans and the rest of nature. They would remind us that our aspirations and our ideals are related to those larger laws that govern all natural things. They might point out that any meaning to life which a person may discover satisfies just because it is in harmony with the laws of nature. But this is a matter of emphasis, of difference in response. For some of us it is the idea of our human isolation and independence which seems particularly meaningful; for others, it is the idea of our interdependence with the nonhuman world. What unites humanists is the conviction that it is to ourselves we must look if we wish to find a master plan by which to shape and give direction to our lives. There is no realm, no force, no personality beyond nature which is the source of meaning and value or which leads us and directs us. Nor is there a special group of religious or philosophical leaders in control of the keys to human virtue and human happiness. We must find them for ourselves.

The reason, of course, why this conviction inspires rather than discourages is confidence that we can do this. We see a worthwhile job to be done and believe that it can be done. Little wonder the humanist feels inspired. A challenge has been given.

For further inspiration the humanist turns to those

fundamental ideas which have given comfort, security, and self-respect.

The sense of unity with all humankind has at times a mystical quality. It can also be exhilarating. The well-loved phrase, "All humans are brothers and sisters," has a particular force, a special ring. The humanist is keenly aware of the plight of *Homo sapiens*, a species which although a part of nature has risen through age-long evolution to a position different from and set apart from other species. A. Eustace Haydon describes humankind as "the only thinking things in all the vastness of time and space. Alone here for a moment between birth and death, a spectacle so pitiful, so tragic and so grand." It is against this stark picture of our isolated place in the world, of our sensitivities, our powers, that the humanist sees all members of our human race wherever they may be—in Port Moresby, in Paris, or in Houston. The humanist identifies with all people and sees their problems as human problems. There is complete and irrevocable commitment to the human adventure.

The humanist is filled with wonder and admiration at the creatures that are human, at their capacity for accomplishment, for sacrifice, at the intricacy and precision of that nervous system which has made it possible for them to stand where they do today in nature's hierarchy. We are convinced that if we use to an ever greater extent our unique capacities for discovery and for cooperation, the future of our race will be a brilliant and a happy one.

Many humanists are moved by the constant realization that all of us are children of nature in every fiber of our being, in every fleeting thought. Both exaltation and humility spring from knowing that we live out our lives within a great enveloping process far larger, far older, than ourselves. Many people feel this is the very heart of their life philosophy. Ruth T. Abbott said: "Our relatedness to the whole of nature is our strength and our source of ethics and our fire in being." Certainly if we consider our fascinating relation to the universe, we are both lifted up and humbled, both disciplined and supported.

Where can one find more astonishing and ironic paradox, more poetry, more mystery than in this relationship? Nature tenderly provides us with the most delicate and precise apparatus for our health and survival. It does the same for the mosquito and the tubercle bacillus. Humankind is lifted to ecstasy by sunset color on mountain peaks and may be sickened with disgust by decaying flesh. Our species feels gratitude for warm sun, full moons, and clean water; we despair before tornadoes and burning droughts. Freed from the necessity of thinking that the natural world was created for human satisfaction or edification, we are able to take nature as it comes. Knowing that humans are fools to expect any special consideration, we are spared the shock of disillusionment and are unencumbered by the notion that nature rewards those we call good and punishes those we call evil. We can be freed from bitterness and can feel a single-minded, wholehearted joy and interest in the beautiful, the orderly, and the awesome aspects of the universe.

Yet for all our calm objectivity we happily confess a connectedness with nature so close that it is almost complete identification. Our most dramatic aesthetic and intellectual triumphs are as much the products of natural processes as the dams of beavers or the hives of bees. For some of us the really exciting and fascinating paradox lies in the fact that for all our efforts to be objective, we cannot set ourselves apart, for in a sense we ourselves are nature. Our meaning of the word "nature" is expanded to include all those most delicate, subtle, and noble of our aspirations that hitherto people have been loath to admit as belonging to the natural world. To us—and this is perhaps the most difficult thing for the non-humanist to understand—the effect of putting humans in nature is not their debasement but the addition to nature of an exciting new dimension.

We look upon evolution of living things as one of the elemental processes in this grand integrated whole. We feel that humans can now play a decisive role in this process. Imagination, our extensive use of symbols, our ability to organize yesterday's experience into tomorrow's dream, set us above all other levels of life. On account of this we are not only able to adapt ourselves to nature but can fashion or recreate parts of the natural world about us. As early as 1916 Cora L. Williams in *Creative Involution* gave an inspiring picture of the human race as master of the evolutionary process. We may yet awake to the possibilities of directing evolution by human knowledge, human good will.

Inspired by a sense of solidarity with our fellows, by bright confidence in the future of the human adventure, and by our relation with nature, the humanist can be eager for the practical challenge with which life confronts us.

For most of us this challenge has lain chiefly in the role that we might play in the building of a better community, a finer nation, a happier world.

Increasing numbers are also thinking of what their rich and varied philosophy means in terms of personal living. When all is said and done, it is the individual's own life and those of others which make changes possible.

Humanism teaches two things which seem at first contradictory but which actually complement and strengthen each other. It teaches us on the one hand how deeply involved we are with nature and with our fellow human beings. On the other hand it encourages us to be independent and self-reliant. We cannot play our part well and responsibly unless we are spiritually weaned. Yet we become more fully developed only through social relationships.

Erich Fromm, Abraham Maslow, Harry A. Overstreet, and others have made clear how important it is for one to be free, to be independent. They show that only as one has self-respect can one have wholesome love for others, can one feel concern for others, can one live adequately with others in our common life.

H. J. Blackham describes the value of active participation in life in *Living as a Humanist*. A humanist says "yes" to life and should be ready and eager for new responsibilities, new human relationships, new experiences of every kind. Humanists take full part in life and at the same time full responsibility for their own past actions. On occasion it may even be strenuous to say "yes" to life. Blackham writes:

> The use and enjoyment of what life in the world offers is not to be had by wanting, nor merely by asking, but only by intelligent, instructed and sustained effort.

An unknown Sanskrit writer expresses the daily challenge of life:

> Listen to the Exhortation of the Dawn!
> Look to this Day!
> For it is Life, the very Life of Life.
> In its brief course lie all the
> Varieties and Realities of your Existence:
>   The Bliss of Growth,
>   The Glory of Action,
>   The Splendour of Beauty;
> For Yesterday is but a Dream,
> And To-morrow is only a Vision,
>   But To-day well lived makes

Every Yesterday a Dream of Happiness,
And every To-morrow a Vision of Hope.
Look well, therefore, to this Day!
Such is the Salutation of the Dawn.

Humanism urges us to recognize in our personal lives the importance of its fundamental method. Human progress as a whole depends on freedom to search for truth. Individual progress also depends, in the same crucial way, on a constant search for truth about oneself. Only as one grows in self-knowledge will one become truly free. Only as one understands one's self can life offer its deeper meanings and be experienced to the full.

Psychologist Rollo May has pointed out that problems of modern men and women center very often in a basic emptiness and in indifference to themselves.

Humanism has a different effect on each person. A clear example of its value for one particular individual has been given by a marketing consultant, Alfred E. Smith, who has told how humanist insights have brightened his life, enabling him to transcend devastating experiences: World War II front-line combat, sudden loss of a cherished eight-year-old daughter, and six years later the tragic death of his wife, leaving him alone to prepare two preschool-age sons for life. A statement he wrote in 1951 was later cited at Phillips Brooks House at Harvard University and printed in the newsletter of the Humanist Association of Massachusetts:

What Being A Humanist Has Done For Me

(1) *Humanism has ended a great aloneness* with which I've had to carry my thoughts and hopes through many years. How wonderful to be able to share with others the quest for truth which had always set me apart from those still complacently caught in the web of traditional beliefs. Just to know that there have been many before me, that there are growing numbers all over the world joined in the same quest ... this gives me new courage and incentive.

(2) *Humanism has given me direction and purpose.* It has dispelled an impatient and often desperate idealism. Humanist discussions and Humanist literature have helped me to know myself better . . . have brought me new perspectives on my life . . . have opened doors to an even wider knowledge of my world and of how I can help to make it better.

(3) *Humanism has given me new values.* I have learned that people and problems are seldom what they seem to be ... that fighting them is futile ... that accepting and understanding them is the only way

to change them. Humanism, with its emphasis on the scientific method, has taught me to seek facts and underlying causes rather than theories and opinions . . . to search out all that the social sciences have discovered to help me . . . to ever test my own judgment as well as that of others . . . and to direct my efforts toward that which is possible within the ideal.

(4) *Humanism has brought me the realization that complete intellectual freedom is vital to human progress . . .* that our first line of advance must be to neutralize with truth the authoritarian forces that seek to enslave the minds of men with superstition, prejudice, obscuration, and propaganda. How glad I am to be part of a movement with this dedication!

(5) *Humanism has helped me to discover the power of love* ... for through its insights I have come to know that achieving the ability to love myself and all others is worth far more than all the moral codes and religious dogmas ever devised. For me, the meaning of Humanism is living love and seeking truth. And because love is limitless and truth is ever-changing,

ever-expanding, I know that Humanism has given me horizons that I will never reach. For that as much as anything I am thankful.

It is clear that humanism offers comfort, support, guidance, inspiration, and a summons. In urging us to know not only the world but ourselves, it offers a quest that will never end.

CHAPTER SIX

Applying Humanism to Personal Problems

The General Approach

Humanism is practical. It motivates us to understand complex situations and to make decisions. If this were not true, humanism could not be the basis for an upbeat, constructive way of life. Although it provides no ready-made formulas, it gives a specific point of view. This view makes it easier to work problems through to solution. It prevents us from creating new problems in the process of meeting old ones. This approach to difficulties is made up of at least two elements.

In the first place it is a certain state of mind. This is one of self-reliance and confidence. People act as they do from perfectly natural causes. As these are natural causes rather than occult ones, there is hope of understanding and perhaps even of controlling them. Success or failure does not depend on the conjunction of Mars and Jupiter, on whether it is our lucky day, or on the configuration of crystals. It depends on whether we can see the chains of cause and effect leading up to the present situation and whether we act on the basis of this knowledge. This is both a disciplined and an encouraging philosophy. We are allowed no transcendental alibis and are freed from insoluble riddles. We are encouraged to feel that there is usually some kind of answer to a problem if we could but find it.

Secondly, this approach involves reliance on a common-sense realistic method. There is willingness to use this method on problems whether routine or serious, clear-cut or vague, practical or emotional. This procedure is basically the thoughtful scientific method. It consists of observing keenly, gathering facts, questioning traditional authority, and carefully checking assumptions. It favors keeping the mind open for new knowledge and being ever reluctant to jump to conclusions.

Fixed convictions, prejudices, and dogmas are tested against experience and the objective findings of others. To a humanist, this can be done whether buying a computer or deciding what one's attitude should be toward an alcoholic relative.

The method requires that when there is time and opportunity to gather information, as much should be collected as seems practicable. On the basis of this, temporary conclusions can be drawn and tested. This course can be followed whether choosing a weight-reducing diet or a political candidate. Where there is no time for this, as often in everyday life, we can at least keep ourselves open for new and better ways of meeting difficulties. (That is, if we meet difficulties!)

Problems Involving Other People

Many of the concerns of everyday life are easily resolved by coupling confidence and curiosity. We must admit, however, that more is usually needed when there are complex relationships with other humans.

A humanist tries to look at problems in social relations from a characteristic perspective, that is, as problems in human happiness, problems in working out what will be best for the people concerned. There is no asking who is or is not right or wrong. As a practical person and as one who recognizes no immutable, hard-and-fast categories of good and evil, the interest is in workable solutions and happy relationships. There are not thoroughly good and thoroughly bad people, merely good and bad behavior; and behavior is likewise judged by its effect on oneself and on others. Situations are approached with confidence in, and openness toward, the people involved. The point of view of others is respected; humanists realize that those others have an equal right to their special slants. The aim is to be non-dogmatic, good humored, in a word, democratic.

Humanists try to have more than a broad perspective. From their mental kits are taken the tool of scientific method which can be used on personal as well as on other problems. This tool is particularly useful when dealing with people, for each of us is psychologically complex and subtly different. We know that each has inherited a different genetic makeup—a slightly different DNA—and that this bundle of characteristic traits has in turn been molded by very different life experiences. We understand also how important it is to recognize that people change. They may react very differently when applying for their first job than when applying for their old-age pension check; they respond differently to a domineering in-law than to an attractive potential mate. The humanist concludes from this that the reasons for people's behavior and changes in behavior are peculiar to each person and to each person's history. They realize that people often have no inkling of why they act as they do—and that friends often know even less.

Here, if ever, is a field where the facts are complex and hidden and where it is difficult to check on suppositions. But armed with their point of view, humanists will humbly be prepared to keep their minds open for new insights. They will refrain from laying down hard-and-fast rules as to how friends and relatives will or should act. They will try to understand rather than to judge.

We can easily summarize this general approach to human relations. It is only by accepting people as they are and by trying to understand them that we can live with them successfully.

Some problems involve clear-cut disagreements, impasses, where the people concerned are at cross purposes. Perhaps relatives are disagreeing as to the distribution of inherited property, or perhaps one neighbor is disputing with another the right to keep a rooster in his backyard. (Let us assume that no one follows the impulse to flee!) A suitable approach to these disagreements would be a good-humored, cheerful concentration on finding some kind of acceptable compromise rather than an insistence that someone is wrong and to blame. Facts would be gathered and communication shared. There would be great interest in finding out what was really "eating" the various people involved and why. There would be willingness to explore several possible solutions and confidence that because of the potential good will of everyone, some mutual understanding could be found.

There are times when one has to make an important decision about another person. A humanistic method consists in bringing into focus what is known about this individual. But it does not necessarily end with this. Because we have faith in people, because we realize that they often mature with experience and learn from their mistakes, because we know that past actions are the result of special circumstances, we do not make hard and inflexible judgments on the basis of past actions alone. As Agnes Hocking, founder of Shady Hill School in Cambridge, Massachusetts, once observed, "One shouldn't make negative comments about personal habits because one never knows whether they are now struggling to change them."

A Practical Example

Let us consider a very simple situation where this flexible point of view is put into practice.

Joanne is in her second year in a college fifty miles

from her hometown. Last week she met John, a guy she had known in high school. He was wearing the uniform of an express company for which he now works.

Joanne hesitated when John asked her for a date. She said she would call him in a couple of days and let him know.

In high school she had liked John and had enjoyed being with him. But John had got into a scrape just after graduation about two years ago. Joanne never was sure what the whole story was but it included his being arrested in a massage parlor which was also a front for drug dealing and prostitution. John had to spend the weekend in jail because his parents did not help by providing bail, saying he should take responsibility for his own actions.

Joanne's parents had forbidden her to see John any more, and had told her he was a good-for-nothing. John's family was not financially well off, and he went to work rather than to college.

Joanne, after this chance meeting, got to thinking whether she should follow her strong emotional desire and make the date. She tried to consider the matter within a broad framework. In her reading she had come across the thought that "nothing is more certain in modern society than that there are no absolutes."

She began to realize that laws and codes and customs as well as institutions are made for humans and not the other way around. And what human good or end would be served by not associating with John?

Then Joanne might have thought of another principle: that we have an inherent capacity for development. We grow and change. What is true at one time may not be so at another.

John, as any other human, is neither all good nor all bad. And, after all, what is meant by good or bad as applied to a person? There is no hard quality of goodness or badness within people. Each person behaves in many different ways—ways which have different consequences.

Joanne probably frowned when she thought for a few moments of a friend whose behavior was not admirable but who nevertheless felt in the clear because she regularly went to confession.

Joanne went to the telephone and made the date.

A few days after the date Joanne's telephone rang and her mother tearfully reported she had heard that Joanne was seen in a mall with John.

Joanne was tempted to shout back some accusations but she caught herself and said that she would explain everything when she came home that weekend.

This gave her additional time to think the matter out and to ponder the varying points of view concerned, including that of her parents. She decided it would be foolishness to talk with her mother about any relativity in morals but she could discuss other phases of the situation.

When the time came, she told her mother how hard it was on the proverbial dog that had been given a bad name. She mentioned that, while John's behavior may have been bad or that the situation may have been different from what appeared, he did have many good qualities, and that people do change.

Because she recognized the human capacity to change she was able to think of John as an individual. "Goodness" and "badness" are verbal abstractions, though useful verbal shorthand for describing how we feel about the behavior of someone else.

This little anecdote about Joanne and John illustrates that the idea of accepting others, of trying to understand people, involves sometimes the taking of a chance. We take the chance that people will act as we, in our friendly confidence, expect them to.

Living with Others

Most of the time disputes or important decisions about people are not our main problems. Our daily concern is our adjustment to those with whom we work and live. Often we want more than merely to get along; we want to build rich and happy friendships. How does a humanist achieve these with a child, a spouse, an in-law, a neighbor, a boss, an employee, yes, even the plumber?

In the humanistic approach, each individual is accepted as he or she is. Given this person with particular habit patterns, particular slants on life, what is a workable way to get along or even achieve a satisfactory relationship?

Another's right to be different would be respected. Realizing the complexities of humankind we would attempt to understand. We would reroute energies from irritation, boredom, or anxiety into efforts to interpret why a cousin is so irritating, a neighbor so boring, or employees so difficult.

Happiness cannot be brought to those you love unless you accept them and understand them. We need to discover why something upsets, frightens, or irritates. If a spouse is nervous on ladders or mountain roads, there is no laughter, criticism, or lecture on how irrational and neurotic the spouse may be. One tries to understand that the attitude may only change slowly, if at all, as its genesis is learned. Change, if any, often lies in giving the feeling of friendly acceptance.

The humanist's acceptance is not passive. One does not see others merely as they are in their present circumstances or state of mind—of irritation, perhaps! One thinks how the individual might be, free from those tensions, hostilities, fears, which influence individuals to act as they do. Also, the individual may be struggling to correct the very habit or behavior.

If the humanist gives others the kind of understanding which has expectation in it, this is encouragement to help a change in attitude for the better.

But it is not enough to accept and to understand the other person; we must try to accept and understand ourselves.

In any real dispute or disagreement the humanist tries

to feel respect for self as for others. There is respect for one's own personal point of view. There is little interest in brooding on whether one is to blame for a past or present difficult situation.

Nothing is of more importance in relationships with others than self-knowledge. Here as nowhere else is the personal value of the scientific method vindicated. One can discover more about self than can ever come in knowing other people. Self-knowledge will produce improvement in relationships more quickly than any insight about others. After an unnecessary quarrel, a reunion with an old friend spoiled by awkwardness on both sides, or after an exasperating inability to stand up for what one believes in front of others, we can ask: Why did I act as I did? This self-examination can be very fruitful.

Living with Oneself

Lying behind the problems of daily life there are often deeper ones, problems of hostility and fear. These are basic attitudes which are reactions to past experiences even dating back to infancy. In this case the search for self-knowledge must be carried on with more persistence and patience.

Within each of us are these fears, tensions, frustrations, and hostilities. It is as though inner demons were urging us to self-destruction. Such is the picture psychiatrists and mystics have often given of humankind.

To free ourselves from these hostilities and fears we

have a humanist orientation which gives self-respect and security, inspiration, and independence. This, of course, is not unique to humanists.

As one comes to be tolerant and understanding of oneself there is increasing personal maturity. Frustrations become fewer, hostilities lessen in intensity. By thinking rationally one is better able to master the inner demons. Creative abilities become released. One more nearly approximates the person one desires to be. Deep inner problems surface and are resolved. Anxiety, boredom, and loneliness become less frequent callers. The individual becomes more of a person.

Julian Huxley shared with others his vision of a world available to those who are sensitive to possibilities. In his book *The Faith of a Humanist,* he explained:

> Many human possibilities are still unrealized save by a few: the possibility of enjoying experiences of transcendent rapture, physical and mystical, aesthetic and religious; or of attaining an inner harmony and peace that puts a man above the cares and worries of daily life. Indeed, man as a species has not realized a fraction of his possibilities of health, physical and mental, and spiritual well-being; of achievement and knowledge, of wisdom and enjoyment; or of satisfaction in participating in worth-while or enduring projects, including that most enduring of all projects, man's further evolution.

CHAPTER SEVEN

Applying Humanism to Social Problems

Humanism as a Spur to Action

Humanism gives a point of view not only valid in personal and psychological matters but in the social and economic situations of our time. It is a stimulus and a guide to making better sense out of our complex, jumbled world.

"Our supreme responsibility is the moral obligation to be intelligent," according to humanist pioneer Oliver L. Reiser. He believed that this is the obligation to know what is going on in the world and to see, insofar as we can, that social change is headed in a right direction. The world is going to continue to change, and those of us sufficiently stout of heart and head can help in the grand undertaking.

If ever there was a point of view which inspires considered action, and the application of theory to practice, it is that of humanism.

Consider these central ideas. We ourselves must take responsibility for making the world a better place in which to live, as there is no being or power, called by whatever name, to whom we can shift this task. We have the means to improve the world through effective use of our human abilities.

This viewpoint badgers us by saying that we can look only to ourselves for help and then encourages us by saying that we do not need any other help. What other articles of faith are so likely to stimulate purposeful action?

The Dream

Humanists are interested in making this a better world. There is no doubt as to that. What kind of a world are they working toward?

They dream of a world in which people can feel self-esteem, find outlets for their energies and opportunities to use their capacities, and have meaningful employment. They seek a world in which reasonable physical and economic needs can be satisfied, a world enriched through cultural diversity. In that world, democratic method and scientific method will be more often merged, for in essence they are relatively similar—both are based on freedom to find and to weigh new courses of action, both are opposed to giving weight to arbitrary prestige or tradition. This improved society will not be a soulless, mechanistic one left to the management of so-called experts.

Most of the citizenry will have the opportunity to take part in selecting capable representatives. The right to be different, to be oneself, will be respected. People will be ready to have more thoughtful and rational methods applied in the educational systems. Courts, hospitals, and other institutions including recreational facilities, will be available to help those requiring their services. Preventive medicine and health care will gain new ascendancy. When social and health workers and social scientists agree on ways of helping individuals and society, it will be the practice to make use of such information. As a result, much of the present mystery shrouding questions as to how humans can be more content, maintain a higher level of personal activity and well-being, and have satisfactory human interrelationships will be dissipated.

The money god and rabid consumerism will have retreated and there will be general appreciation of that ideal whereby free time for creative expression or recreation is valued as highly as mere pieces of silver.

Freedom for All

Whether or not one considers humans as pivocs (poor innocent victims of circumstance) is largely a matter of temperament. We are beset on every side with forces which crowd in on us. In the January 1, 1949, *New Yorker*, the liking and respect for the individual which is at the very heart of humanism was vividly expressed:

> In 1949, the individual was busy fighting
> to retain his status. The tide was strongly
> against him. He fights for the security
> of his person, for the freedom of his

conscience, for the right to speak and the right to listen and the right not to listen when the speaking is too dull or too loud. Everywhere the individual feels the state crowding him, or the corporation crowding him, or the church crowding him, or the home crowding him. The enigma today is not the energy locked in one atom but the strength stored in a single man—the ability of this man to survive when he is always half submerged in something bigger (but not really) than he is. Here, at the end of 1948, we stretch out our mitt to this fellow.

Is it not a source for wonder that humans are so magnificently resilient? Deep within us is the urge to affect circumstance, to change. The suppression of this impulse leads to personal unhappiness and dis-ease, and, in a way, to a blocking of the evolutionary process. There are psychological limits beyond which society and the environment should not press or crowd an individual.

Above all else, perhaps, humanists believe in freedom; they believe that not only is it a human's right to speak and act freely—within the limits of public safety—but that freedom is the means by which one can develop one's potentialities.

Behind the humanist's convictions is the faith that life can offer much contentment and be a satisfying experience for those allowed self-respect and freedom.

For some humanists the right of each person to be different, and to be comfortable in this difference, is the essence of their philosophy. For others, the emphasis is on how one's behavior and actions affect other people.

The humanist is a profound believer in protecting the rights of all individuals, in seeing that they have equal civil liberties. Whereas there are wide differences of opinion as to the degree to which the state should regulate the lives of citizens—in such matters as regulation of private industry, labor, and price and wage controls— there is no real disagreement among them over the need of giving each citizen as much freedom as is practically possible. A wide range of kinds of government can be useful to their citizens. So long as others are not harmed, individuals should express themselves as they choose, read or watch what they choose.

We are reminded here of what Henry David Thoreau said: "If a man does not keep pace with his companions, perhaps it is because he hears a different drummer. Let him step to the music he hears."

And remember Aldous Huxley's observation: "Among many other things, democracy is non-interfering, is leaving other people alone."

Humanists are in agreement that no strong country, not even the United States, should take advantage of its strength to dictate to a weaker nation how it should run its affairs. The Western world has no right to assume that it has been ordained in the heavens to be the leader and teacher of the Eastern or Southern worlds. The humanist recognizes aspects of all cultures as appropriate ways in which societies have built up reaction patterns to life.

Social Action

Humanism's active concern for social reforms has sometimes led to its even being called applied Christianity. An evangelical Christian and a humanist often share similar emotions and practical goals in social action, though the philosophical underpinnings are different. It is noteworthy that usually where there is a vigorous effort to effect any basic social reform, such as a court case in defense of someone's civil liberties, there is at least one acknowledged humanist actively involved.

Rational thinking is basic in the humanist philosophy. Before turning to see how this approach might be employed by someone deeply concerned with social problems, let us consider some of the activities in which many humanists are now at work. It is only fair to mention that some of these programs and causes are not approved or actively participated in by all humanists.

(1) They encourage scientific research into the underlying reasons for social tensions and personal ill health. They encourage the widespread use of new scientific knowledge. This interest in science for humanity might be considered particularly far-reaching and characteristic.

(2) They work for civil liberties. They believe that those who would limit certain phases of our civil rights, who would spread suspicion, distrust, and dissension among ourselves, are often unaware of the harm which results from their methods. Each individual of the United States, each individual of the world, has the right to life, liberty, and the pursuit of happiness. It is the preservation and extension of these rights for which humanists fight.

(3) They work to lessen racial antagonisms and prejudices. They consider the barriers which separate people to be primarily psychological and open to change. Education of many kinds is needed to combat the ignorance which lies behind racial hatreds and jealousies.

(4) They are apt to give support to the United Nations and to the work of its divisions including the United Nations Educational, Scientific, and Cultural Organization, the World Health Organization, and the Food and Agriculture Organization. The United Nations is not regarded as perfect but as having accomplished great good in

keeping open avenues of communication and bridges among nations, and in keeping alive certain ideals. The strengthening of the United Nations will go a long way toward lessening international tensions.

(5) In the United States they work for the continued separation of church and state. To them this separation is an underlying concept in many countries, and they exert every effort to keep it so. In public schools in the United States there are instances where children have been separated for special released-time religious classes, and it has been tragic to see the mounting hostilities and class consciousness which have resulted. Children discover sometimes for the first time that they are Protestant, Catholic, Jewish, Muslim, or without religious affiliation. When a public school program focuses on one type of religion, the atmosphere of democratic community can be destroyed.

(6) They encourage all efforts to increase the world's food supply. Growth, preservation, and distribution are equally important. It is disheartening to see food surpluses destroyed when elsewhere

hunger stalks. Any controlled economy which destroys these surpluses is not functioning for the benefit of all humankind. Attention is given to distributing leftover and outdated restaurant and grocery store surpluses.

(7) They work to extend understanding of the values of family planning and birth control. They do not believe in arbitrarily controlled parenthood but in the extension to fathers and to mothers the right to plan their own families, to have children when they can best take care of them and give them love and security. The right and ability to plan one's own family has not as yet become universal.

(8) They work to improve health services of all kinds, to encourage preventive medicine, to use centuries-old practices and substances from many cultures, and to awaken people to a recognition of the importance of psychological factors, including stress. A little understanding and intelligent preventive therapy can avert much mental and physical suffering and family tragedy.

(9) They tend to have a vigorous interest in establishing and strengthening free public school systems. They resist attempts of special groups to influence public education, whether they be political or religious, business or labor. Opportunities for all children—boys and girls—should be offered on the basis of their abilities and needs and not on the basis of the color of their skin or the social background of their parents. Universal literacy and education are global concerns.

(10) They believe meaningful employment for young people is essential and recognize the shortcomings of overwrought materialistic consumerism.

(11) They are concerned to provide education for girls and broader opportunities for all women.

(12) They work for environmental integrity with realization that our global home has to be maintained so that it can be habitable in future centuries.

These twelve fields have one thing in common. They help individuals to enjoy greater freedom and well-being. Yet not every humanist entirely agrees on these or any other courses of social action.

It is not specific social action that is the heart of the humanist approach to social problems. Problems are endless and vary in different cultures and locations. And some problems influence other problems. For example, population increase hastens the diminishing of some natural resources; climate stresses and changes hasten the pollution of the earth, water, and sky. Moreover, people of goodwill can disagree on the best responses. So the heart of the humanist approach is to be found in the application of rational methods. This is what is fundamental.

Humanist Principles That Bear on Social Problems

Let us pause for a moment and consider four principles underlying social action.

(1) Humanists believe it is the welfare of the individual and society which counts. By this standard a humanist may examine the appropriateness of laws, governments, churches, customs, and other institutions. All institutions are measured in terms of the quality of life they promote. They are successful as they make for better living for humans.

(2) Humanists express their conviction in

the value of individuals through a strong stand on human equality. They believe that no gender, race, nationality, class, or other group "is inherently qualified to ride herd over any other." This does not mean that in some areas, cultural and economic patterns do not lead to differences. Greater equality in educational and living opportunities lessen these differences.

(3) Humanists are concerned that we all should be free to think, free to speak as we like so long as it doesn't harm others, and free to act independently. They are concerned that no one be "pushed around." They are opposed to totalitarianisms that impose arbitrary authority on individual thought and conduct. They are mindful of what Woodrow Wilson said in New York in 1912:

> The history of liberty is a history of the limitations of governmental power, not the increase of it. When we resist… concentration of power, we are resisting the powers of death, because concentration of power is what always precedes the destruction of human liberties.

(4) Humanists are convinced that through cooperation and the intelligent use of knowledge, we can create a more satisfactory life for all.

These convictions come naturally, of course, to those who believe that there is intrinsic value in human feelings and that the happiness and the welfare of others are goals. If this life on earth is all we can look forward to, it is unthinkable that we should not make life for ourselves and others relatively satisfying and free from anxieties. By the use of our resources we can partially solve many of our problems. This has become a firm hope, almost a slogan.

And because of faith in the human ability to solve problems, it is natural that the humanist lives vigorously. We know we must and can depend on the intelligent cooperation of individuals of good will to continue to remove conditions and change attitudes which breed poverty, under-employment, hunger, war, violence, disease, fear, and prejudice.

Tackling a Social Problem

Humanists, in tackling a social problem, strive to use the scientific-democratic method. They also envision, while remaining open-minded, certain goals which they can look to as a guide and check. These would be the well-being of humankind and concern for individuals as individuals. There are no more important goals over and beyond these.

To start with, information and points of view are considered. Those that seem the most relevant are set apart. Our old friend the scientific method is in high gear.

No matter how emotionally charged the atmosphere, no matter how "close to home" the issue, the humanist would attempt to look at it freshly, honestly, objectively. When necessary, desirable, and possible, there would be an attempt to search out the opinions and experience of those on differing sides of the controversy.

They would try to weigh the effects of bias, of limited experience. If one or another solution had been tried elsewhere, they would try to ascertain how it had worked in practice. For example, let us say the desirability of changing tariffs is under discussion. They would consider what actually happened when tariffs were raised or lowered by our own and other nations. Or again, in considering the treatment of persons, they would check to find out how other states and counties handle rehabilitation projects, disciplinary measures, and parole problems.

What have been the results of the particular policy in other places?

They would attempt to remain open-minded, flexible, to face squarely the truth that what works at one place, at one time, may not work well at another place, at another time. They would be conscious of the complexity of our human life in the twenty-first century. They would not generalize on such a matter, say, as government ownership of gas, water, and electric companies. They would see that circumstances might make it an excellent policy in one country and a very questionable one in another which has a different culture and political bureaucracy.

Because of this flexibility, this dislike of generalizing, of jumping to conclusions, humanists would not be blocked or upset, for example, by hearing someone allege that such and such a policy is "un-American" or "un-German." Our interest would be in considering what the results of such a policy might be. How would they affect citizens in different cultures?

We know that words are dangerous though necessary tools—meaning different things to different people. Sometimes words, or the meanings hastily applied to them, serve to discourage us from carefully looking into what is happening, or may happen. Tensions mount when dog-matists confront cat-egorists.

What about those cases where the humanist has little time to study or reflect, little opportunity to observe at first hand?

In those cases, we are inclined to suspend judgment, to make no pronouncement at all. We will have respect for those who have taken time and pains to investigate, or who are through training and experience fitted to make predictions more objectively. We would not go to the extreme of Ronald Reagan, who noted during his presidency that he was not an expert in matters of philosophy and ethics and so he would defer to the judgment of the pope.

At this point, someone may wonder whether humanists believe they have a monopoly on use of a kind heart, common sense, and rationality in social affairs. Certainly not.

They may, however, have a kind of advantage. For they hold in mind two things when attacking a problem: the well-being of all individuals and the necessity of using the scientific method. People generally tend to employ but one or the other of these—or have other goals entirely.

Faced with making a judgment about a political regime, a humanist would ask: Are the citizens, as individuals, subservient to any person, any class, any institution? Is there any group of citizens cut off from participating in the life of the country because of national origin or membership in any particular class or race?
So far as political party allegiance in our own country is concerned, educator and humanist pioneer William Heard Kilpatrick wrote:

> A humanist may belong to any reputable party, provided that in his acceptance of this party affiliation he consistently maintains his respect for human personality and its full development, his acceptance of democratic freedom and equality joined with commitment to the common good and his determination to find out by the

free play of intelligence what to think and do as he faces the successive situations of life.

Many individuals have summarized their outlook on social issues. In 1989 Ted Turner listed ten "Voluntary Initiatives" which might have been written by most other humanists:

> (1) I promise to have love and respect for the planet earth and living things thereon, especially my fellow species— humankind.

> (2) I promise to treat all persons every- where with dignity, respect, and friendliness.

> (3) I promise to have no more than two children, or no more than my nation suggests.

> (4) I promise to use my best efforts to save what is left of our natural world in its untouched state and to restore damaged or destroyed areas where practical.

> (5) I pledge to use as little nonrenewable resources as possible.

(6) I pledge to use as little toxic chemicals, pesticides, and other poisons as possible and to work for their reduction by others.

(7) I promise to contribute to those less fortunate than myself, to help them become self-sufficient and enjoy the benefits of a decent life, including clean air and water, adequate food and health care, housing, education, and individual rights.

(8) I reject the use of force, in particular military force, and back United Nations arbitration of international disputes.

(9) I support the total elimination of all nuclear, chemical, and biological weapons of mass destruction.

(10) I support the United Nations and its efforts to collectively improve the conditions of the planet.

Turner became the Humanist of the Year of the American Humanist Association in 1990.

CHAPTER EIGHT

The Development of Organization

Although many humanists throughout the world do not belong to any organization with the humanist name, groups have formed on six continents. The International Humanist and Ethical Union, based in London, represents upwards of four million humanists organized in over 100 national organizations in forty countries. It is an international non-governmental organization with Special Consultative Status at the United Nations, General Consultative Status at the UN International Children's Educational Fund (UNICEF) and the Council of Europe, and maintains operational relations with the UN Educational, Scientific, and Cultural Organization (UNESCO). The organization also has offices in New York City for the IHEU-Appignani Center for Bioethics and works closely with the European Union. The IHEU celebrated its fiftieth anniversary in 2002 by conferring the International Humanist Award on Nobel Laureate in Economics Amartya Sen at its World Humanist Congress in Amsterdam.

Forerunners of Modern Humanist Organizations

Around 1850, Auguste Comte, a pioneer French

sociologist formulated a "religion of humanity" based on his intellectual philosophy of Positivism. He wrote: "Every subversive scheme now afloat has either originated in Monotheism or has received its sanction" and "there are now but two camps: the camp of reaction and anarchy, which acknowledges more or less distinctly the direction of God; the camp of construction and progress, which is wholly devoted to Humanity." Positivist clubs and congregations were formed in Europe and the Americas. In 1881 the Church of Positivism was established in Brazil. It continues to this day and Comte's slogan, "Order and Progress," is part of the Brazilian national flag. Comte's humanistic religion was warmly regarded by William James and F. C. S. Schiller.

Apparently independent of Comte, in London, England, the Humanistic Religious Association was formed in 1853. Declaring, "We have emancipated ourselves from the ancient compulsory dogmas, myths and ceremonies borrowed of old from Asia and still pervading the ruling churches of our age," these early religious humanists gathered democratically for cultural and social meetings and provided for the education of their children and assistance to members in need. Then, more than a decade later, in 1866, freethinking social reformers united under the leadership of Charles Bradlaugh to form the National Secular Society, a more activist organization that would, within a century become fully identified with humanism. Meanwhile, in Germany in 1859, a new liberal Christian denomination, the Bund Freireligioser Gemeinden Deutschlands (Federation of Free Religious Congregations of Germany) was established. It, too, would become humanist a century later.

In 1867, in response to a temporary turn toward Christian creedalism in the American Unitarian Association, dissenters founded the Free Religious Association. Organized in Boston, Massachusetts, under the leadership of Ralph Waldo Emerson, it appealed not only to theological radicals among Unitarians, but also to non-Christian religious liberals. Among its later luminaries were Rabbi Isaac M. Wise, organizer of Reform Judaism, and Felix Adler, founder of Ethical Culture. The association, however, never moved beyond what it would eventually call *humanistic theism*, and it ceased to exist by the outbreak of World War I.

During the late nineteenth century the brilliant works of Robert Green Ingersoll and Mark Twain loosened the hold of religion for millions of people.

In 1876, Felix Adler established the New York Society for Ethical Culture as an organization devoted to ethical behavior of individuals, rather than to creedal statements. Both ritual and prayer were excluded from meetings and social service became a central focus. Its underlying philosophy was a neo-Kantian, transcendental idealism. Soon other ethical societies were set up in Chicago, Philadelphia, and St. Louis. Together with Unitarians, settlement houses were established. Such activities gave emphasis to the development of social work as a profession. The movement later inspired the development of the Legal Aid Society, the National Association for the Advancement of Colored People, and other major American reform efforts.

Influenced by Ethical Culture, Moncure Conway, an American minister of a Unitarian chapel in London, England, began guiding his congregation in a specifically ethical direction until, in 1887, his church became the South Place Ethical Society. In 1896, the International Ethical Union was established and, for over four decades, it united Ethical Culturists in the United States with those in the United Kingdom, Germany, Switzerland, Austria, and New Zealand.

Though Ethical Culture did not fully identify itself with a non-transcendental humanism until the 1950s, it was indirectly involved in the adoption of *humanism* as a modern term.

In 1915, a Positivist, Frederick James Gould, writing in a magazine published by the British Ethical Societies, used the word to denote a belief and trust in human effort. Reading the article, John H. Dietrich, a Unitarian minister in Minneapolis, Minnesota, was influenced to view *humanism* as the best name for his new, fully naturalistic, religious outlook.

This came at a time when dissent was strong within American Unitarianism—a struggle between ministers, on one side, who wanted a creed that would exclude both nontheists and other post-Christian dissenters from the denomination and ministers, on the other side, who opposed such creedalism. Among the dissenters were two others who had used the term *humanism* in a modern sense: Edward Howard Griggs, author of *The New Humanism: Studies in Personal and Social Development*, published in 1899, and Frank Carleton Doan, author of *Religion and the Modern Mind*, published in 1909. But it wasn't until Dietrich and another forthright nontheist, Curtis W. Reese, combined their efforts at the Western Unitarian Conference of 1917, that the humanist movement got underway in both name and substance. A year later, academic philosopher Roy Wood Sellars published *The Next Step in Religion*, a book that added vitality to religious humanism.

As other philosophers (particularly John Dewey, Charles Morris, Max Otto, Oliver L. Reiser, and later Sidney Hook and Corliss Lamont) fed the growing stream of ideas, humanism became more widely accepted as a term in Unitarian, Universalist, Ethical Culture, and Quaker congregations, as well as among freethinkers and thoughtful academics.

Simultaneously, literary humanism, with a different emphasis as featured by Paul Elmer More and Irving Babbitt, was widely discussed early in the twentieth century.

Early Humanist Groups

With interest in the philosophy aroused, a number of Unitarian professors and seminarians at the University of Chicago and Meadville Seminary came together in

1927 to form the Humanist Fellowship. The next year they launched *The New Humanist*, the first journal devoted exclusively to serving the young movement. That same year, evolutionary scientist Julian Huxley, in *Religion Without Revelation*, set forth the principles of humanism in a popular fashion.

In 1929, Charles Francis Potter, a Unitarian minister who had served as Clarence Darrow's biblical expert at the Scopes "Monkey" Trial, left his denomination and founded the First Humanist Society of New York. There he and Sherman Wakefield offered humanism as "a new faith for a new age." This stimulated wide interest.

Also that year, in Bangalore, India—apparently unconnected with similar activity in the West—a humanist club was established with Colonel Raja Jai Prithvi Bahadur Singh of Nepal as its first president. Rabindranath Tagore was among its members. Elsewhere in India, various rationalist and freethought groups had been functioning since the late 1800s. Out of this diverse effort grew Self-Respect, a highly influential social and political reform movement founded in Madras in 1925 by Periyar. Openly nontheistic, the Self-Respect movement opposed the caste system and Hindu beliefs, supported human rights, and promoted science. Periyar later identified his efforts with humanism.

The depression year 1933 was when thirty-four intellectual leaders formulated and signed a document called "A Humanist Manifesto," which was first published in *The New Humanist*. Unitarian ministers

Raymond B. Bragg and Edwin H. Wilson took the lead in this initiative. Today, that document, though not a creed, is sometimes considered dated, but its basic analysis and aspirations are acknowledged as appropriate for the twentieth and twenty-first centuries.

In California in 1939, a group of Quaker humanists, led by Lowell H. Coate, broke away from their denomination and, at a meeting of the First Universalist Church of Los Angeles, established the Humanist Society of Friends. Inspired by the Humanist Manifesto, they offered "a scientific religion for a scientific age and a universal ethics which shall end war." Meanwhile, a similarly inspired intercollegiate science seminar, whose coordinators were H.G. Burns, J. T. Stockdale, Daniel Levinson, and one of the authors (Lloyd), became the Los Angeles Scientific Humanist Group. The writings of George Bernard Shaw had influenced some of the members. During this time humanist Bertrand Russell came to teach at the University of California at Los Angeles. Gerald Heard and Aldous Huxley, also from England, as well as German novelist Thomas Mann and philosopher Hans Reichenbach, added to the rich humanist presence which is still felt in Southern California today.

Following World War II, three prominent humanists became the first directors of major divisions of the United Nations: Julian Huxley of UNESCO, Brock Chisholm of the World Health Organization, and John Boyd-Orr of the Food and Agricultural Organization.

Huxley, in particular, called for a global humanist vision. In his monograph, *UNESCO: Its Purpose and Its Philosophy*, he pointed out the necessity of transcending traditional philosophies, theologies, and political-economic doctrines and the importance of recognizing the evolutionary basis of culture. Science, he said, needs to be integrated with other human activities, and the general philosophy of UNESCO should be a scientific humanism, global in extent and evolutionary in background. But Huxley's effort was only partially successful; representatives holding onto nationalistic and traditional views blocked and jettisoned the forthrightly humanist aspects of his proposal.

In postwar Europe, humanist secular organizations sprang up in a number of countries, particularly Belgium, Italy, and the Netherlands. In India, M. N. Roy launched the politically focused Radical Humanist Movement, which for some years had a large impact; and Gora, an associate of Mohandas Gandhi, expanded the Atheist Centre, a humanistic social service institution he had established in 1940. Shortly thereafter Jawaharlal Nehru, a thoroughgoing humanist, became India's leader.

Around this time a number of small beginnings were forming in Africa. The authors visited population workers and humanists in 1959 in Nigeria including Samuel Etu, an educator whose school library had a complete set of the published writings of Robert Ingersoll. One of the authors (Mary) was scheduled to speak to the humanist group in Lagos. Our automobile broke down in central

Nigeria and we hitchhiked, arriving with only an hour to spare. To Mary's surprise only three current members showed up with the explanation given that the majority of the members were in prison for advocating social changes.

In the United Kingdom, Harold Blackham of the British Ethical Union began discussing with humanists throughout the world the desirability of establishing closer international cooperation. Together with Professor Jaap van Praag of the Netherlands and others, meetings were held at the Municipal University of Amsterdam in August 1952. Chaired by Julian Huxley, it hosted over two hundred humanists from around the world, including Gilbert Murray of the United Kingdom, Jerome Nathanson from the United States, and V.M. Tarkunde of India. The authors were present and one (Mary) became a member of the board of directors of the International Humanist and Ethical Union, the organization that emerged from the gathering.

Among the first actions of the IHEU were decisions to support the World Federation of Mental Health, meeting in Brussels, Belgium, and the World Conference on Planned Parenthood, meeting in Bombay, India. After considerable thoughtful discussion, a declaration setting forth the fundamentals of modern ethical humanism was adopted.

This declaration offers humanism as "a third way out of the present crisis of civilization," being an alternative to revealed religion on the one hand and totalitarian systems on the other. Humanism supports democracy, not only in the political realm but in "all human relationships." It "seeks to use science creatively, not destructively. . . . Science gives the means but science itself does not propose ends. . . . Humanism is ethical," affirming human dignity and "the right of the individual to the greatest possible freedom of development compatible with the rights of others." In so doing, humanism "rejects totalitarian attempts to perfect the machine in order to obtain immediate gains at the cost of human values." It "insists that personal liberty is an end that must be combined with social responsibility in order that it shall not be sacrificed to the improvement of material conditions." And it is "a way of life, aiming at the maximum possible fulfillment, through the cultivation of ethical and creative living."

CHAPTER NINE

The American Humanist Association

One of the founding organizations of the International Humanist and Ethical Union, the American Humanist Association, is sufficiently important as an example in the development of organized humanism that its individual history is worth recalling.

By the beginning of 1935, the Humanist Fellowship had evolved into the Humanist Press Association. In 1936, however, its publication, *The New Humanist*, folded. So a newsletter, *The Humanist Bulletin*, under the editorship of Edwin H. Wilson, was launched by the same organization. That was discontinued in 1941 to make way for a new journal, *The Humanist*, and a new name, the American Humanist Association. This Association's first four presidents were all signers of "A Humanist Manifesto." One of these, Curtis W. Reese, had, with John H. Dietrich, started the humanist movement within the United States in 1917.

Throughout the 1940s and 50s, humanists, many of whom did not know of the AHA or care to belong to an organization, were involved in numerous civil liberty, birth control, and environmental protection cases often tried in court. The most prominent of these humanists was Corliss Lamont, philosopher and author of *The Philosophy of Humanism*, who successfully stood up to the House Un-American Activities Committee and Senator Joseph McCarthy. Another was Vashti McCollum, a housewife who later became president of the AHA. Her U.S. Supreme Court victory in *McCollum v. Board of Education* established that American public schools must be religiously neutral. On the environmental front, there was interest in the value of restraint and the damage done by runaway population growth—matters which are still insufficiently acted upon around the world.

During the middle 1950s, Hermann J. Muller, a Nobel Laureate in genetics, served as president. He, together with Chauncey Leake and Anatol Rapoport, approached the American Association for the Advancement of Science, suggesting that the AHA could appropriately be its philosophical branch. The AAAS declined the proposal on the basis that the AHA's membership did not include a high enough percentage of PhDs. Psychologists and psychiatrists including Erich Fromm, Abraham Maslow, Albert Ellis, B.F. Skinner, Carl Rogers, and Rudolph Dreikers all wrote extensively on humanism. One might call it their basic philosophy. Collectively their efforts gave a naturalistic slant to understanding and improving mental health and social well-being.

Mid-century, the AHA worked internationally

through Karl Sax, Margaret Sanger, and William Vogt to slow population growth and became the first national membership organization to stand up for the right of a woman to have an abortion. Many of the leading abortion-law reform groups of the time had a significant humanist leadership—in particular, the Religious Coalition for Abortion Rights (now the Religious Coalition for Reproductive Choice) and the National Association for the Repeal of Abortion Laws (now NARAL Pro-Choice America). Also during this period, the AHA worked with the American Ethical Union to establish the rights of nontheistic conscientious objectors to opt out of combat service.

Ernest Morgan, humanist co-founder of the Arthur Morgan School, published *A Manual of Simple Burial* that soon inspired the development of memorial and cooperative burial societies nationwide—alternatives to the traditional mortuary-controlled system of burial.

Edwin H. Wilson, executive director of the AHA, as a side endeavor established the Fellowship of Religious Humanists (now the HUUmanists) to keep humanism alive and thriving within the newly merged Unitarian and Universalist denominations. In 1970, philosopher Paul Kurtz, editor of *The Humanist*, launched Prometheus Books as a humanist publishing house. It has grown to become the world's leading publisher of freethought, humanist, and skeptical books.

"Humanist Manifesto II," with the editorial guidance of Edwin H. Wilson, Roy Fairfield, and Paul Kurtz, was issued by the AHA in 1973, receiving front-page coverage in the *New York Times*. This new declaration modified the optimism of the earlier document, acknowledging that "Nazism has shown the depths of brutality of which humanity is capable," and expanded the application of humanist ideas, including commenting on a broad range of social concerns.

The next year, the AHA established the National Commission for Beneficent Euthanasia which issued the groundbreaking statement, "A Plea for Beneficent Euthanasia." This position paper, signed by medical, legal, and religious leaders, called for "a more enlightened public opinion to transcend traditional taboos and move in the direction of a compassionate view toward needless suffering in dying." Today these ideas are a part of public discussion.

In 1975, the AHA solidified its position regarding the pseudoscience of astrology and again earned media attention with the publication of "Objections to Astrology." This humanist consumer-advocacy statement was signed by 186 scientists, including eighteen Nobel Prize winners.

Early in 1976, under the guidance of sexologists Lester A. Kirkendall and Sol Gordon, the AHA issued "A New Bill of Sexual Rights and Responsibilities," prompting *Time* magazine to remark that humanists celebrate responsible sexual freedom after centuries of bondage to church and state. Today most traditional religious denominations continue to grapple with the sexual issues humanists came to terms with decades ago.

In the wake of articles in *The Humanist* which were critical of pseudoscience, the AHA established in May of 1976 the Committee for the Scientific Investigation of Claims of the Paranormal. Through its membership of humanist leaders and scientists, CSICOP launched the *Skeptical Inquirer*, challenged pseudoscientific claims, and exposed much of the faulty experimentation, frauds, and fallacies of "psychic research." Now called the Committee for Skeptical Inquiry, it is a dynamic, independent consumer-information organization.

Early the next year, the AHA established itself as a major force in the creation-evolution controversy by issuing "A Statement Affirming Evolution as a Principle of Science" and sending copies of it to every major school district in the country.

In September 1977, the AHA took a vigorous stand against age discrimination in matters of employment and retirement. "A Declaration for Older Persons" was signed by members of Congress, labor leaders, housewives, business executives, and religious leaders, stirring further media attention. Many of the principles expressed in this statement have since become codified into law.

The 1980s was a period of vicious attacks on humanism by the religious right. Humanists responded with public debates, media appearances, articles, press conferences, lobbying, and in a few instances legal action. The high profile of these attacks has lessened, given the scandals that later rocked televangelism, but the skills honed during these turbulent years continue to help humanist leaders actively thwart new radical-right initiatives. Bringing new vigor to this effort was another AHA spin-off, the Council for Democratic and Secular Humanism (now the Council for Secular Humanism), founded in 1980 by Paul Kurtz. Meanwhile, the journal *Creation/Evolution*—the only periodical in the world devoted exclusively to answering the religious right's creationist arguments—was launched by AHA executive director Fred Edwords. (Seventeen years later it would become part of a newer publication, *Reports of the National Center for Science Education*, still published today.) In 1985, world-renowned author Isaac Asimov became president of the AHA, serving until his death in 1992.

As humanists and the general public expressed a growing need for a nontheistic alternative in addiction care, the AHA made Rational Recovery a corporate division and launched it into the national limelight. Lois and Jack Trimpey had originated this unique substance-abuse program, originally based on the rational-emotive behavior therapy of Albert Ellis. Later, that effort branched into two independent humanistic programs, Rational Recovery and SMART Recovery.

In 1990 the AHA, with the inspired leadership of Maxine Negri, arranged a friendly merging with the Humanist Society of Friends, thereby reinvigorating the humanist counselor and celebrant program that makes humanist weddings, memorial services, and personal counseling available to a wide range of people seeking alternatives to traditional ceremonies and pastoral care. In that same year, humanist counselor James T. McCollum, son of Vashti McCollum, performed the first humanist wedding service ever conducted at West Point Military Academy.

The AHA returned to Chicago, the city of its roots, to celebrate its 50th anniversary in 1991. Lester R. Brown, president of the Worldwatch Institute, and Werner Fornos, president of the Population Institute, were honored there as humanists of the year. *Star Trek* creator and longtime humanist Gene Roddenberry was recognized with the Humanist Arts Award.

In 1994 the AHA began blazing new trails in cyberspace. Humanist bulletin boards, chat rooms, e-mail lists, newsgroups, special interest groups, and websites began springing up, introducing humanism to a wider audience.

In 1995 the AHA, with the creative efforts of its president Edd Doerr, joined with a variety of secular organizations and religious groups in issuing "Religion in the Public Schools: A Joint Statement of Current Law," which influenced policy decisions nationwide and prompted favorable comment by then President of the United States Bill Clinton.

In 2000 the AHA moved its headquarters to Washington DC and began building its influence among political leaders and the nation's leading activist organizations. A boost in its media outreach led to widespread awareness of humanist opinions on the critical issues of the day. And the release in 2003 of "Humanism and its Aspirations: Humanist Manifesto III" led to wider awareness of basic humanist principles. The document has been signed by twenty-two Nobel Laureates, among numerous other luminaries. More recently, through the leadership of Executive Director Roy Speckhardt, the AHA has expanded its operations, creating the Appignani Humanist Legal Center and the Kochhar Humanist Education Center.

Over the years the Association has stimulated the founding of chapters, alliances, and conferences to bring together people who share viewpoints and interests. Leaders of groups with innovative activities have included Arthur Jackson in San Jose and Tom Ferrick and Greg Epstein at Harvard University. The AHA is a member organization of the Secular Coalition for America, managed by Executive Director Lori Lipman Brown.

Among the Association's programs have been essay contests for those under thirty. In the 1950s both *Harper's* magazine and *Galaxy* were co-sponsors. Many winners are having socially significant careers. Two of these, Annie Laurie Gaylor and Timothy J. Madigan, are leaders in their fields. The contest continues today in *The Humanist*.

The Association's Feminist Caucus has benefited from

the unique efforts of Meg Bowman, Rosemary Matson, and Patricia Willis. Many others have in varying capacities shown by their lifestance how to make effective contributions to society: Barbara Dority, Beverley Earles, Gloria Steinem, and Carol Wintermute.

The Association has enjoyed the intellectual leadership of unique and capable individuals. Over the years Edd Doerr, a past president and student of religious liberty in crisis, has maintained accurate reporting of moves to destroy the separation of church and state. Gerald Larue and Robert Price have been depended on to provide understanding of archeological findings relevant to biblical and other religious texts. From the Ozarks Lester Mondale provided stimulating musings on living simply. Ethelbert Haskins opened new understanding of how the crises in Afro-American leadership could be constructively resolved. Delos McKown, Konstantin Kolenda, Paul Edwards, Anthony Flew, Roger Greeley, and Joseph E. Barnhart have highlighted philosophical insights and understanding. Philosophical explorations have recently expanded through the AHA's philosophical journal, *Essays in the Philosophy of Humanism*, edited by Marian Hillar.

Throughout its history the association's primary publication, *The Humanist*, has served as a major periodical, bringing humanist viewpoints and interpretations to bear on leading issues of personal and social concern. In the 1940s and 50s, for example, it carved intellectual frontiers by publishing material that showed how perceptions clinging to verbal bases limit common sense. Alfred Korzybski, Anatol Rapoport, Harry Lee Maynard, Allen Walker Read, and S.I. Hayakawa have been the leading humanists giving attention to this revolutionary approach in thinking and understanding known as general semantics.

In the 1950s leading physicists, sociologists, psychologists, and historians confronted in the pages of *The Humanist* such theoretical issues as science and human values, global human rights, and the problems of traditional systems of faith. Then, in the 1960s and 70s, as America was undergoing major social change, the magazine turned to addressing justice, racism, ways to reduce poverty, student unrest, communes, war, abortion, women's rights, changing moral values, and the new cults of unreason.

Attention was given to the criminal justice system and how the building and staffing of prisons has degenerated into an employment and construction growth industry. Years ago *The Humanist* described how the criminal justice system can be effectively humanized. Less than ten percent of prisoners are habitually incorrigible before incarceration and these individuals can be identified and should be separated from society. Keeping many offenders in prison breaks their ties with family and friends, throws them out of the mainstreams of education and employment, and leads to lives of underachievement and despair. This is not just costly to the individuals but to our whole society.

In the 1980s *The Humanist* brought new attention to the consequences of uncontrolled immigration whereby individuals from other lands with limited skills compete with American citizens for jobs. The magazine also exposed the problem that population pressures such as under-employment are linked to gender discrimination and the traditional worldwide subjugation of women.

Three individuals, who eventually will be looked back on as significant twentieth century pioneers, have had frequent access to the pages of *The Humanist*. Fran P. Hosken, perhaps more than any other person, has kept alive and intellectually cross-fertilized the situation of women throughout the world. Her publication *WIN News* (Women's International Network) gives current news of women's concerns ranging from slavery, genital mutilation, labor, and gender discrimination to childbirth and healthy children.

Another enlightening thrust has come from Riane Eisler, whose study of how societies have historically become dominated and hence limited by males. She is best known for her landmark book *The Chalice and the Blade*.

Almost as significant as the work of Margaret Sanger is that of Stephen Mumford, who has outlined how inappropriate practices can lead to lopsided surges in population and the quality of living. He has revealed how the World Health Organization has knuckled under to the Vatican and accordingly largely neglects birth control programs. Together with health professionals in several nations, his pioneering effort is making available quinicrine, a relatively simple, safe, inexpensive, non-surgical female contraceptive.

As the religious right began its attacks, *The Humanist* reassured readers of the value of common sense and self respect. An example of this was an exposé by Gerard Straub, former producer of Pat Robertson's *700 Club*.

Articles also focused on the humanization of health care. Work concentrating on the endeavors of Nathan, Ilene, and Robert Pritikin and Linus Pauling in the 1980s were strongly denounced by editors of medical journals who have now come to recognize the need for and value of preventive medical practices, including lowering fat intake and increasing that of herbs, vitamins, and minerals; practicing meditation and adopting positive mental attitudes.

Then, in the 1990s, increased attention was given to applying humanism directly to urgent issues of civil liberties and human rights. Exposé articles appeared on such subjects as the drug war, federal crime policies, employer misuse of "honesty tests," government attempts to censor the Internet, church-state issues affecting the Boy Scouts of America, religious influence on national elections, international prostitution, the global landmine problem, and even the use of sweatshops in the toy industry. Among the social commentators who wrote for *The Humanist* were Dan Rather, Noam Chomsky, Faye Wattleton, Barbara Trent, Justice Harry Blackmun, and Howard Zinn.

The Humanist carried articles showing how less materialistic addictions can lead to a better sense of well-being. The quality of life was shown to be more important than the clogging possession-accumulation habit. Attention was given to how housing for those in need is often blocked by bureaucratic rules and regulations and union restrictions.

In the first decade of the twenty-first century, *The Humanist* has critiqued the nation's wars as well as policies on torture and government surveillance, challenged World Trade Organization policies, was awarded for its coverage of the sweatshop scandal, educated readers on global warming, analyzed problems with electronic voting machines, exposed government aid to religion, debunked faith-based prison programs, demystified Islam, explored transhumanism, supported same-sex marriage, and introduced "Humanist Manifesto III." Well-known contributors have included Ann Druyan, Amy Goodman, Jim Hightower, Wendy Kaminer, Kate Michelman, Jonathan Miller, Robin Morgan, Ralph Nader, Joyce Carol Oates, Steven Pinker, Salman Rushdie, William F. Schulz, Steven Weinberg, and Edward O. Wilson.

One of the roles of the AHA throughout its history has been to inject mainstream society with energizing ideas and stimulate the development of new endeavors. As such, the Association serves to some extent as a "pilot organization," an institution that initiates pioneering social programs that sometimes take on a life of their own. This helps explain why humanism in the United States has an influence out of proportion to its number of organized adherents.

Overall the AHA helps to provide the satisfaction and even joy of having a philosophy which lets one adjust to change and is in tune with knowledge. It provides added power to the desire to do right. Humanists recognize that unkindnesses and iniquities toward other people will not be remedied in an afterlife by a supreme being.

Annually the Association recognizes artists, pioneers and heroines who have made significant contributions to human betterment. Starting in 1953 a Humanist of the Year was designated, with the first honor going to Anton J. Carlson, a physiologist and former president of the American Association for the Advancement of Science. Subsequent recipients of this prestigious award have been the following humanists:

Arthur F. Bentley	Andrei Sakharov
Jonas E. Salk	Brock Chisholm
James P. Warbasse	Carl Sagan
Corliss Lamont	Leo Szilard
C. Judson Herrick	Helen Caldicott
Margaret E. Kuhn	Linus Pauling
Margaret Sanger	Lester A. Kirkendall
Edwin H. Wilson	Julian Huxley
Oscar Riddle	Isaac Asimov

Hermann J. Muller

John Kenneth Galbraith

Carl Rogers

Faye Wattleton

Hudson Hoagland

Margaret Atwood

Erich Fromm

Leo Pfeffer

Abraham H. Maslow

Gerald A. Larue

Benjamin Spock

Ted Turner

R. Buckminster Fuller

Werner Fornos

A. Philip Randolph

Lester R. Brown

Albert Ellis

Kurt Vonnegut

B.F. Skinner

Richard D. Lamm

Thomas Szasz

Lloyd and Mary Morain

Joseph Fletcher

Ashley Montagu

Mary Calderone

Richard Dawkins

Henry Morgentaler

Alice Walker

Betty Friedan

Barbara Ehrenreich

Edward O. Wilson

William F. Schulz

Stephen Jay Gould

Steven Weinberg

Sherwin T. Wine

Daniel C. Dennett

Murray Gell-Mann

Steven Pinker

Joyce Carol Oates

Pete Stark

CHAPTER TEN

The Great Adventure

Humanism: a Joyous View

As indicated in the introduction, before reading this book you may have been among the growing number of Americans who did not realize they were humanists. But now, with new awareness of the humanist lifestance, you may be discovering that here is a worldview in harmony with your intelligence that can give you a thoroughly consistent basis for meaning, moral values, and inspiration.

Humanism offers an alternative to religious faith, one that is in tune with the revolutionary, growing knowledge of our physical and mental worlds. It is both rational and compassionate and provides a new source of joy and strength. Humanism encourages service to others and offers the sense of community and connectedness that is consistent with our social nature as human beings. It also provides personal security while preparing us to live more comfortably in a changing society. It does so by adding the elements of discovery and adventure, providing clearer purpose and energizing us as we move our lives forward.

How to Decide Whether You Are a Humanist

So, have you been a humanist, perhaps without even knowing it? To help you make up your own mind we offer the following guidelines:

(1) Do you believe that we will continue to learn more about the past, present, and future of planet earth and its inhabitants?

(2) Do you believe that humans are a part of nature and that there is no god or supernatural power especially concerned for their welfare?

(3) Do you believe that religions' sacred scriptures and ethical and moral systems were the creations of mortals and that these have served different purposes at different times and places?

(4) Do you believe that the kind of life we live and the helpful and just relationship that we have with other humans is of primary importance?

(5) Do you feel that our environment needs to be taken care of and protected for future generations?

(6) Do you frequently experience joy and comfort and an undefined mystic sense from the realization that you are a part of nature and of all that lives?

(7) Do you believe that the meaning of life is that which we give to it?

(8) Do you recognize that many philosophical questions such as, "What is the meaning of life?" and "Why am I here?" are irrelevant when our existence and experience are viewed as processes within the totality of nature?

If you answer "yes" to most of these questions you can classify yourself as a humanist, for you view humankind in naturalistic and humanistic terms. You have faith in our future here on earth and believe the highest goal for human endeavor is a better world for all.

Are you willing to consider new evidence of any kind and in every field of human thought and behavior, even though this may lead to a revision of some of your most cherished beliefs? We cannot see how anyone who is consistent in belief in a theistic religion or a non-naturalistic philosophy would be able to answer this in the affirmative. Humanists can.

For Sober Reflection

We all know that in some ways our inner resources are not keeping pace with external ones. Each year sees more machines and devices bringing added leisure to large numbers of the world's people. Yet little seems to be achieved in helping these people to be basically happier, wiser, or more considerate of others. Even among those with countless information age gadgets and abundant leisure there is often ennui, a sense of futility and sometimes worthlessness. Furthermore, in most countries large segments of the population lack many basic needs, including meaningful work, and this is reflected in the persisting number of poor.

What is wrong? The explanation most frequently given is that we do not follow Christianity, Islam, Buddhism, or whatever the religion happens to be. Say the theologically-minded Christians: "If only people would come to know God and Jesus, if only they would accept Him on faith and not question or hold back!" Understandably, religious fundamentalists often feel disenchanted with present-day society and advocate a return to imagined past practices. Not unsurprisingly, most of them have limited knowledge of historic brutality, misery, and depressions.

The humanist looks at the situation and possible solution differently. There is appreciation and partial acceptance of the values of the historical ethical codes. It is noted, however, that these very old codes contain views on slavery, race, castes and classes, women, and

other significant matters which are not acceptable to
contemporary educated men and women. Then, too,
there are countless situations upon which the old codes
do not provide guidance. The humanist feels hopeful
that our inner growth will be greater when the same
procedures that have made scientific achievements
possible are used by ourselves in our own personal
development and social relations. The remedy is
in looking forward, not backward, in observation
and experience, in free imagination, in studying
consequences of action, and not in dependence upon
revelation and tradition. To date there has been no
nation which has put into general practice the scientific
method—the humanist method. Whole nations have
been Christianized or galvanized behind other major
philosophies and religions. Most of the Christian ideals
are admirable, but more than the voice of revelation is
needed to make them living realities.

What Humanism Gives Us

As we have seen, humanism serves as both an inspiring
alternative to faith and as a very adequate philosophy
for daily living. Truly this sparkling way of life is richly
rewarding and deeply satisfying.

We see ourselves as a dynamic part of nature,
responding to the same laws as do other creatures. We
observe the working of these so-called natural laws,
finding no need to set ourselves apart from the world or
to project our various human purposes or plans onto the

grand cosmic scheme of things.

Depressing negatives have been turned into challenging positives. What if we are the result of evolutionary change from lower animals? We can feel pride and responsibility in being the highest form of life that has as yet evolved.

What if the vast universe is neutral toward our human hopes, our human ideals? We have a sense of belonging and are still free to carve out our own plans, set our own standards. We also recognize that each of us is born with individual limitations. However, each of us is free to give whatever meaning we wish to our life. Moreover, with increasing knowledge we learn more of nature's laws and how to cooperate with them more fully. The ethical ideals of the great religions can more nearly become living realities.

Many find in this alternative to faith a satisfying vision and philosophy which does not run counter to their common sense knowledge of the world. For them new vistas have been opened. New possibilities for human cooperation in making a heaven on earth have been presented. Many intellectually mature adults and questioning, enterprising youth are accepting the challenge and opportunity to develop and participate in this alternative to faith. They recognize that the traditional religions do not fit the reality of today's information and biotechnological age. When there are sufficient numbers of humanists in the world, isn't it reasonable to assume there will be positive changes?

From now until then there may well be hard and difficult periods. Yet in going forward, anyone can join in this greatest of human adventures.

Albert Schweitzer, man of international good will and recipient of the Nobel Peace Prize for 1952, said:

> The world thinks it must raise itself above humanism; that it must look for a more profound spirituality. It has taken a false road. Humanism in all its simplicity is the only genuine spirituality. Only ethics and religion which include in themselves the humanitarian ideal have true value. And humanism is the most precious result of rational medi[t]ation upon our existence and that of the world.

There is satisfaction in discovering that in heart and mind one is a humanist. Many doubts, uncertainties and stresses vanish. This adventure into understanding the nature of beliefs and knowledge makes living more worthwhile and inspirational. Gone is any sense of aloneness, for now one feels at home with at least a few like-minded people in every part of the world.

The Humanist Philosophy in Perspective

by Fred Edwords

What sort of philosophy is humanism? To listen to its detractors, one would imagine it to be a doctrinaire collection of social goals justified by an arbitrary and dogmatic materialist-atheist worldview. Leaders of the religious right often say that humanism starts with the belief that there is no god; that evolution is the cornerstone of the humanist philosophy; that all humanists believe in situation ethics, euthanasia, and the right to suicide; and that the primary goal of humanism is the establishment of a one-world government.

And, indeed, most humanists are nontheistic, have a non-absolutist approach to ethics, support death with dignity, and value global thinking. But such views are not central to the philosophy. To understand just where humanism begins, as well as discover where such ideas fit into the overall structure, it is necessary to present humanism as a hierarchy of positions. Certain basic principles need to be set forth first—those ideas that unite all humanists and form the foundation of the philosophy. Once this is done, humanist conclusions about the world can follow—conclusions which, by the nature of scientific inquiry, must be tentative.

Then, after that groundwork has been laid, appropriate social policies can be recommended, recognizing the differences of opinion that exist within the humanist community. From this approach people can see humanism in perspective—and in a way that reveals its nondogmatic and self-correcting nature.

The central ideas of humanism, then, can be organized into a practical structure along the aforementioned lines. Even though all humanists don't communicate the philosophy in this way, it is fair to say that most humanists will recognize this presentation as accurate.

Basic Principles

1. We humanists think for ourselves as individuals. There is no area of thought that we are afraid to explore, to challenge, to question, or to doubt. We feel free to inquire and then to agree or disagree with any given claim. We are unwilling to follow a doctrine or adopt a set of beliefs or values that does not convince us personally. We seek to take responsibility for our decisions and conclusions, and this necessitates having control over them. Through this unshackled spirit of free inquiry, new knowledge and new ways of looking at ourselves and the world can be acquired. Without it we are left in ignorance and, subsequently, are unable to improve upon our condition.

2. We make reasoned decisions because our experience with approaches that abandon reason convinces us that such approaches are inadequate and often

counterproductive for the realization of human goals. We find that when reason is abandoned there is no "court of appeal" where differences of opinion can be settled. We find instead that any belief is possible if one lets oneself be aided by arbitrary faith, authority, revelation, religious experience, altered states of consciousness, or other substitutes for reason and evidence. Therefore, in matters of belief, we find that reason, when applied to the evidence of our senses and our accumulated knowledge, is our most reliable guide for understanding the world and for making our choices.

3. We base our understanding of the world on what we can perceive with our senses and comprehend with our minds. Anything that is said to make sense should make sense to us as humans; else there is no reason for it to be the basis of our decisions and actions. Supposed transcendent knowledge or intuitions that are said to reach beyond human comprehension cannot instruct us because we cannot relate concretely to them. The way in which humans accept supposed transcendent or religious knowledge is by arbitrarily taking a leap of faith and abandoning reason and the senses. We find this course unacceptable, since all the supposed absolute moral rules that are adopted as a result of this arbitrary leap are themselves rendered arbitrary by the baselessness of the leap itself. Furthermore, there is no rational way to test the validity or truth of transcendent or religious knowledge or to comprehend the incomprehensible. As a result, we are committed to the position that the only thing that can be called knowledge is that which is

firmly grounded in the realm of human understanding and verification.

4. Though we take a strict position on what constitutes knowledge, we are not critical of the sources of ideas. Often intuitive feelings, hunches, speculation, and flashes of inspiration prove to be excellent sources of novel approaches, new ways of looking at things, new discoveries, and new concepts. We do not disparage those ideas derived from religious experience, altered states of consciousness, or the emotions; we merely declare that testing these ideas against reality is the only way to determine their validity as knowledge.

5. Human knowledge is not perfect. We recognize that the tools for testing knowledge--the human senses and human reason—are fallible, thus rendering tentative all our knowledge and scientific conclusions about the nature of the world. What is true for our scientific conclusions is even more so for our moral choices and social policies; these latter are subject to continual revision in the light of both the fallible and tentative nature of our knowledge and constant shifts in social conditions.

To many this will seem an insecure foundation upon which to erect a philosophy. But because it deals honestly with the world, we believe it to be the most secure foundation possible. Efforts to base philosophies on superhuman sources and transcendent "realities" in order to provide a greater feeling of security only end up creating illusions about the world which then result in errors when these illusions become the basis for decisions and social policies. We humanists wish to avoid these costly errors and, thus, have committed ourselves to facing life as it is and to the hard work that such an honest approach entails. We have willingly sacrificed the lure of an easy security offered by simplistic systems in order to take an active part in the painstaking effort to build our understanding of the world and thereby contribute to the solution of the problems that have plagued humanity through the ages.

6. We maintain that human values make sense only in the context of human life. A supposed nonhumanlike existence after death cannot, then, be included as part of the environment in which our values must operate. The here-and-now physical world of our senses is the world that is relevant for our ethical concerns, our goals, and our aspirations. We therefore place our values wholly within this context. Were we to do otherwise—to place our values in the wider context of a merely hoped-for extension of the reality we know—we might find ourselves either foregoing our real interests in the pursuit of imaginary ones or trying to relate human needs here to a very different set of nonhuman needs elsewhere. We will not sacrifice the ethical good life here unless it can be demonstrated that there is another life elsewhere that necessitates a shift in our attention and that this other life bears some relation and commonality with this one.

7. We ground our ethical decisions and ideals in human need and concern as opposed to the alleged needs and concerns of supposed deities or other transcendent entities or powers. We measure the value of a given choice by how it affects human life, and in this we include our individual selves, our families, our society, and the peoples of the earth. If higher powers are found to exist, powers to which we must respond, we will still base our response on human need and interest in any relationship with these powers. This is because all philosophies and religions we know are created by humans and cannot, in the final analysis, avoid the built-in bias of a human perspective. This human perspective limits us to human ways of comprehending the world and to human drives and aspirations as motive forces.

8. We practice our ethics in a living context rather than an ideal one. Though ethics are ideals, ideals can only serve as guidelines in life situations. This is why we oppose absolutistic moral systems that attempt to rigidly apply ideal moral values as if the world were itself ideal. We recognize that conflicts and moral dilemmas do occur and that moral choices are often difficult and cannot be derived from simplistic yardsticks and rules of thumb. Moral choices often involve hard thinking, diligent gathering of information about the situation at hand, careful consideration of immediate and future consequences, and weighing of alternatives. Living life in a manner that promotes the good, or even knowing what choices are good, is not always easy. Thus, when

we declare our commitment to a humanist approach to ethics, we are expressing our willingness to do the intensive thinking and work that moral living in a complex world entails.

Tentative Conclusions about the World

1. Our planet revolves around a medium-sized star, which is located near the edge of an average-sized galaxy of as many as 300 billion stars, which is part of a galaxy group consisting of more than thirty other galaxies, which is part of an expanding universe that, while consisting mostly of cold, dark space, also contains perhaps one hundred billion galaxies in addition to our own. Our species has existed only a very short time on the earth, and the earth itself has existed only a short time in the history of our galaxy. Our existence is thus an incredibly minuscule and brief part of a much larger picture.

In light of this, we find it curious that, in the absence of direct evidence, religious thinkers can conclude that the universe or some creative power beyond the universe is concerned with our well-being or future. From all appearances it seems more logical to conclude that it is only we who are concerned for our well-being and future.

2. Human beings are neither entirely unique from other forms of life nor are they the final product of some planned scheme of development. The available evidence shows

that humans are made from the same building blocks from which other life forms are made and are subject to the same sorts of natural pressures. All life forms are constructed from the same basic elements, the same sorts of atoms, as are nonliving substances, and these atoms are made of subatomic particles that have been recycled through many cosmic events before becoming part of us or our world. Humans are the current result of a long series of natural evolutionary changes, but not the only result or the final one. Continuous change can be expected to affect ourselves, other life forms, and the cosmos as a whole. There appears to be no ultimate beginning or end to this process.

3. There is no compelling evidence to justify the belief that the human mind is distinct and separable from the human brain, which is itself a part of the body. All that we know about the personality indicates that every part of it is subject to change caused by physical disease, injury, and death. Thus there are insufficient grounds for belief in a soul or some form of life after death

4. The basic motivations that determine our values are ultimately rooted in our biology and early experiences. This is because our values are based upon our needs, interests, and desires which, themselves, often relate to the survival of our species. As humans we are capable of coming to agreement on basic values because we most often share the same needs, interests, and desires and because we share the same planetary environment.

Theoretically, then, it is possible to develop a scientifically based system of ethics once enough is known about basic human needs, drives, motivations, and characteristics and once reason is consistently applied toward the meeting of human needs and the development of human capacities. In the meantime human ethics, laws, social systems, and religions will remain a part of the ongoing trial-and-error efforts of humans to discover better ways to live.

5. When people are left largely free to pursue their own interests and goals, to think and speak for themselves, to develop their abilities, and to operate in a social setting that promotes liberty, the number of beneficial discoveries and accomplishments increases and humanity moves further toward the goal of greater self-understanding, better laws, better institutions, and a good life.

Current Positions on Social Policy

1. As humanists who are committed to free inquiry and who see the value of social systems that promote liberty, we encourage the development of individual autonomy. In this context, we support such freedoms and rights as religious freedom, church-state separation, freedom of speech and the press, freedom of association (including sexual freedom, the right to marriage and divorce, and the right to alternative family structures), a right to birth control and abortion, and the right to voluntary euthanasia.

2. As humanists who understand that humans are social animals and need both the protections and restraints provided by effective social organization, we support those laws that protect the innocent, deal effectively with the guilty, and secure the survival of the needy. We desire a system of criminal justice that is swift and fair, ignoring neither the perpetrator of crime nor the victim, and ignoring neither deterrence nor rehabilitation in the goals of penalization. However, not all crimes or disputes between people must be settled by courts of law. A different approach involving conflict mediation, wherein opposing parties come to mutual agreements, also has our support.

3. As humanists who see potential in people at all levels of society, we encourage an extension of participatory democracy so that decision-making becomes more decentralized and thus involves more people. We look forward to widespread participation in the decision-making process in areas such as the family, the school, the workplace, institutions, and government. In this context we see no place for prejudice on the basis of race, nationality, color, sex, sexual orientation, gender identification, age, political persuasion, religion, or philosophy. And we see every basis for the promotion of equal opportunity in the economy and in universal education.

4. As humanists who realize that all humans share common needs in a common planetary environment,

we support the current trend toward more global consciousness. We realize that effective environmental programs require international cooperation. We know that only international negotiation toward arms reduction will make the world secure from the threat of thermonuclear or biological war. We see the necessity for worldwide education on population growth control as a means of securing a comfortable place for everyone. And we perceive the value in international communication and exchange of information, whether that communication and exchange involve political ideas, ideological viewpoints, science, technology, culture, or the arts.

5. As humanists who value human creativity and human reason and who have seen the benefits of science and technology, we are decidedly willing to take part in the new scientific and technological developments around us. We are encouraged rather than fearful about biotechnology, alternative energy, and information technology, and we recognize that attempts to reject these developments or to prevent their wide application will not stop them. Such efforts will merely place them in the hands of other persons or nations for their exploitation. To exercise our moral influence on the new technologies, to have our voice heard, we must take part in these revolutions as they occur.

6. As humanists who see life and human history as a great adventure, we seek new worlds to explore, new facts to uncover, new avenues for artistic expression,

new solutions to old problems, and new feelings to experience. We sometimes feel driven in our quest, and it is participation in this quest that gives our lives meaning and makes beneficial discoveries possible. Our goals as a species are open ended. As a result, we will never be without purpose.

Conclusion

Humanists, in approaching life from a human perspective, start with human ways of comprehending the world and the goal of meeting human needs. These lead to tentative conclusions about the world and relevant social policies. Because human knowledge must be amended from time to time, and because situations constantly change, human choices must change as well. This renders the current positions on social policy the most adaptable part of the humanist philosophy. As a result, most humanists find it easier to agree on basic principles than on tentative conclusions about the world, but easier to agree on both than on social policies. Clarity on this point will erase many prevalent misunderstandings about humanism.

This appendix is an edited version (1998 and 2007) of an article of the same title that appeared in the January/February 1984 issue of *The Humanist* magazine. Fred Edwords is the director of communications for the American Humanist Association and former editor of *The Humanist*.

Index of Names

JOIN THE MOVEMENT!

Become a Member of the American Humanist Association

Why belong to an organization? Because it's only through organized numbers and a strong central voice that change can be effected, liberties protected, and rights ensured—and gained.

The **American Humanist Association** is an organization of people working for the advancement of humanism and humanistic change.

Strategically located in Washington DC, the AHA actively educates the public about humanism, brings humanists together for mutual support and action, defends the civil liberties and constitutional freedoms of humanists—indeed of all peoples— and leads both local and national humanist organizations toward progressive social change.

You are invited to join the AHA to find inspiration in this view of life and actively share in its promise for a better world.

Try our $35.00 Special introductory rate! As an AHA member you will receive:

- Subscription to *The Humanist* magazine and *Free Mind* newsletter
- Invitations to and discounts on AHA literature, conferences and seminars, and all specialty items
- Full voting privileges so you can direct the course of humanism

Join the AHA today! Just fill in the form to the right, add your check or credit card number, and return it to:

American Humanist Association
1777 T Street, NW
Washington, DC 20009-7125

You may also join online at **www.americanhumanist.org** (just click "Join" in the upper-right corner), via e-mail at info@americanhumanist. org, or on the phone by calling toll-free at 1-800-837-3792.